All about
the Dachshund

This little dog with three inch clearance
   Presents a ludicrous appearance,
His legs are bowed, his feet turn out,
   He gives us much to laugh about

He's two dogs long, a half dog high,
   In spite of which he's quick and spry:
So at his funny build don't smirk
   It's perfect for his special work.

For Dachshund plays a hero's role
   In going down a badger's hole;
A badger is a savage fighter,
   A vicious scratcher and a biter.

And folks who call him 'dash-hound' show
   Their ignorance and do not know
That 'dox-hoont' is his proper name
   In Germany from whence he came.

David Newell – *Boston Herald*
with thanks

All about
the Dachshund

KATHARINE RAINE

PELHAM BOOKS/STEPHEN GREENE PRESS

PELHAM BOOKS LTD/STEPHEN GREENE PRESS

Published by the Penguin Group
27 Wrights Lane, London W8 5TZ
Viking Penguin Inc., 40 West 23rd Street, New York, New York 10010, USA
The Stephen Greene Press, Inc., 15 Muzzey Street, Lexington, Massachusetts 02173, USA
Penguin Books Australia Ltd, Ringwood, Victoria, Australia
Penguin Books Canada Limited, 2801 John Street, Markham, Ontario, Canada L3R 1B4
Penguin Books (NZ) Ltd, 182–190 Wairau Road, Auckland 10, New Zealand

Penguin Books Ltd, Registered Offices: Harmondsworth, Middlesex, England

First published 1972, revised 1980 and this edition first published 1989

A CIP catalogue record for this book is available from the British Library

ISBN 0–7207–1816–3

Typeset in 11/12pt Plantin and
Printed and bound by Butler & Tanner Ltd,
Frome and London

Contents

Illustrations

Photographs

Photographic credits

John L. Ashbey 147; K. Barkleigh-Shute 134 (below), 135, 136; Rich Bergman 143 (top); Laurie Bloomfield 148; Callea 145; Terry Dorizas 138; Thomas Fall 56 (top); Fountain 14, 19, 63, 126; H. F. McFarlane 43; *Milton Keynes Gazette* 52; L. Mitchell 15; Diane Pearce 30, 32, 42; Don Petrulis 142; Anne Roslin-Williams 29, 41, 56; R. & L. Skelton 139; Michael M. Trafford 135 (below), 137; Robing Twigg 136; Missy Yuhl 141.

Figures

Acknowledgements

This book would be incomplete without the assistance of, and contributions by, many friends and colleagues and to them I record my appreciation and grateful thanks.

In particular to Mrs Ally Molony, for her translation of Dr Schneider Leyer's *Der Dachshund*.

To Frau Anneliese Wurm for outstanding research into the pedigree of Ch. Zeus vom Schwarenberg.

To Mr Harry Spira, M.R.C.V.S., for his article on virus infection in bitches.

For her article on the dapple Dachshund, to Madame Suzanne de Bernes.

To Mrs Barbara Pugh, for her article on whelping and puppy rearing.

To Neil S. Kay for his chapter on Dachshunds in South Africa.

To the Kennel Club for permission to reproduce the Breed Standard and to the American Kennel Club for permission to reproduce the American Breed Standard.

1 The History of the Breed

Old time documents tempt one to ascribe to the Dachshund a pedigree dating back to ancient Egypt. It is certain that by chance, mutation and finally also by recognised breeding, our own breed has been evolved from the oldest known breeds of dogs.

In old German documents there is mention of the Tracking Dog, and of the 'Bibarhunt', a predecessor of the 'Teckel'. With the start of the sixteenth century we find in documents repeated use of the designations 'Earth Dog', 'Little Burrow Dog', 'Little Burrower', 'Badger Digger', 'Badger Creeper' and 'Dachsel'.

Woodcuts of the years 1576–82 often show these cross-bred dogs with Terrier heads and docked tails on a lengthy Dachshund body. In a work of 1719 there appear two copper plates of a 'Badger Digger' and a 'Badger Killer' that could be said to resemble a Dachshund.

At the end of the seventeenth century the 'Badger Fighter' is described as 'a peculiar, low crook-legged species', whilst in 1848 Teckels became known to hunting historians of that period and were described as follows: 'a good looking Dachshund is of long and low construction, the back arched, belly drawn up weasel fashion, the chest deep, the neck long and strong, with the canine teeth interlocking closely. The eye expressive and spirited, the tail fine and not carried too gaily. The hindlegs more stiff and straight than is usually the case in other dogs. The forelegs strong and muscular, not crooked, but only with the broad strong feet turned outwards. The colour uniformly yellow or black, with yellow extremities and eyebrows.'

Definitely till 1748 the smooth-haired variety of Dachshund was the offspring of crossing the Miniature French Pointer (or Bracke) with the Pinscher (or Vermin Killer). Following the French Revolution in 1789 there were those, amongst the emigrés, who fled to Germany or Austria with their dogs. The French Basset at that time resembled the Dachshund closely, the Basset being smaller and the Dachshund heavier, the Basset being either white in ground colour, red, or black and tan, with white patches on chest and feet. The two breeds were crossed and the resulting pups, if long-legged, became Dachsbracke, if shorter-legged, short-eared and with pointed muzzle, they became the Dachshund.

In 1896 Dr Emil Ilgner undertook the task of setting forth a comprehensive treatise on the breed. In this book he represented the

Dachsbracke as being of equal merit. This dog was started in southern Austria for the express purpose of tracking animals which had been wounded and would otherwise have been lost in wooded and mountainous country. In appearance it resembled a big and powerful Dachshund about a foot high, short-haired, deep-chested, with heavy bow forelegs and large splayed forefeet.

Dr Ilgner, the founder of numerous Dachshund societies both at home and abroad, made sure that the Dachshund would never lack for support. His work was followed up by Engelman, a native of Bavaria, who all his life followed with his Dachshunds his favourite form of hunting fox and badger.

The Dachshund has been written about, described, and praised in all hunting journals over the years, and goes to prove how firmly the Teckel has established himself in the life and heart of mankind. For in no other breed is there such a perfect blend of character and craft, humour and deep philosophical gravity, nonsense and most valuable hunting sense as in our Dachshunds.

The Teckel owed its first introduction into this country to the Prince Consort, who, around 1845, imported several specimens of this then unfamiliar breed from Prince Edward of Saxe-Weimar. These first imports appear to have been kept at Windsor where, we are told, they were frequently to be seen in the Windsor Forest coverts accompanying their Royal master on pheasant shooting expeditions. The keen interest shown by Queen Victoria and her Consort in the 'alien hound', as it was described by a contemporary writer, naturally focused attention on the breed and it was not long before several commoners followed the Royal example by bringing over some of these short-legged, long-bodied little dogs from Germany. These canine curiosities became much sought after by ladies of fashion, to be aired and paraded in Hyde Park.

Dachshunds, directly descended from those received from Saxe-Weimar, were bred in the Royal Kennels through the reign of Queen Victoria, and during his mother's lifetime, the Prince of Wales, later King Edward VII, both owned and showed a team of his own. At the Crystal Palace Show of 1875, where two classes were scheduled for Dachshunds, the Prince of Wales exhibited four speci-mens and won first prize in the class for black and tans, the second prize being won by a bitch bred by the Queen. Dachshunds were favourites of that great dog lover Queen Alexandra, wife of King Edward.

The Dachshund in his English home unfortunately became not only a fashionable dog but a house dog. As by nature he was already of comical appearance, the breeders of those years gradually exaggerated these characteristics and he became still lower, still longer and still heavier. This was followed by the beer-barrel Teckel who appeared in every comic paper of the day.

In the year 1881 the English Dachshund Club was formed, and from that date the nucleus of breeders began a systematic import of stock, gradually improving the type and reducing the size.

The Long Hairs first made their appearance in England around 1920. They had been known in Germany since the first Teckel Stud Book had been produced in 1890. In that year five of this variety had been entered. The registration forty-five years later had risen to over 1,000 and by 1949 had outstripped the other two varieties of Standards, with the Smooths in third place.

The Wire Hairs were not popular in this country for many years after the formation of the Dachshund Club, though a dog had been imported in 1888. In Germany, their registrations in the first Stud Book of 1890 were only three, but by 1938 they had risen to the leading variety.

Amongst the earliest importations, the great authority on the breed, Mr John Sayer, had purchased a dog, Racker von der Ecke, in 1903 who possessed the qualities which were lacking in many English-bred dogs of that time. This dog excelled in legs, feet and bone, had a clean-cut outline and general soundness. The dog was widely used at stud and produced some good pups. Mr Sayer mated him to a small chocolate dapple bitch of his own and from this mating sired a silver dapple dog, later to make history as the first dapple Champion under the name of Spotted Dog. Racker was used by Major Hayward, the owner of the famous 'Honey' strain, and indeed had many of the best bitches to him.

Following the 1914–18 war, the Dachshund lost much ground, a senseless form of retaliation against anything that was German having resulted in much persecution of the breed. Over the years this little dog had come to be the symbol of the corpulent Teuton and amongst the unbalanced and weak-minded, nothing was bad enough for him. Added to the fact of his German origin was the difficulty in procuring food for dogs (numbers had been put down in all breeds).

The end of the war found the Dachshund population not only to be low in numbers but of very poor quality and sadly in need of new blood. This was supplied by the import of an outstanding dog in Theo von Neumarkt (German registered as Asbecks Theo) a black and tan born in 1917, who being born during the war was ineligible for exhibition in England. He was widely used at stud before coming to this country and had champion progeny amongst the inmates of the von Luitpoldsheim kennel – this famous affix being prominent in this country twenty years later with the importation of Zeus vom Schwarenberg.

Theo's most famous son was Remagan Max, born in Germany in 1920. Max was deep red in colour, of medium size, a game, hard, very sound dog. His appearance in the English show ring was spectacular. Never exhibited at any but Championship events, he won eighteen Certificates in his seven years of competition. Max came to England at a time when the variety was suffering severely from the effect of the war years. Type was very varied, size was unstable and unsoundness was the rule rather than the exception. Max's good qualities were quickly appreciated and his services were much in demand. All sorts of bitches were sent to him over a period of six years and he had the knack of getting good progeny from most of them. His offspring were soon occupying the leading positions in the prize lists. Max possessed not only great showmanship and the ability to transmit his excellence, but had the true Dachshund temperament, in that he was active, game and fearless, quick-witted and devoted to those he knew. In all, a great dog.

The next dog to make his mark on the English stock was Faust von Forstenburg. First exhibited in 1924 he became a Champion eighteen months later. He had done much winning in the country of his birth (Germany), but on account of his love of hunting was difficult to keep in show condition. He proved of special value in mating to Remagan Max stock and soon sired several Champions.

In 1930 the late Madame Rikovsky imported a dog who was quickly to make a great reputation as a stud force, this being the dog soon to become Ch. Wolf von Birkenschloss. His breeding can be traced through his great-granddam to the dam of Ch. Max. Before leaving Germany he had been classified 'excellent' and soon found his feet in our show rings, quickly becoming a Champion. Before his advent in England, the stock here had improved vastly, thanks to the careful imports previously mentioned. The heads, back-lines and movements, together with overall quality, were on the up-grade. Size was too large, however, shoulders were incorrect, and feet called for attention. Wolf was immediately recognised as being a type somewhat different to that recognized by English breeders. He was a small red dog, very compactly and strongly built and looked capable of standing up to, and enjoying, a hard day's work. He excelled in general soundness, shoulder placement, hind-quarters and feet, the points in which so many of the English dogs failed. Mated to bitches carrying the blood of Theo von Neumarkt, Ch. Remagan Max and Ch. Faust von Forstenburg, he proved extremely prepotent in passing on his own qualities, and in so doing proved to be the foundation of the well known Firs line prominent in the 1930s.

Madame Rikovsky later imported the clear red Kunz Schneid who was much used at stud, in particular founding the Grunwald red line through Sally of Sunnyflowers.

Other imports of consequence at this time were Ch. Emmo von Rautenschild and Darling von Fallthor, who were both red. Following these dogs came an import of considerable merit not only to the Smooth variety but also, through a long-haired ancestor, to the Longs. The dog in question soon received his crowning Certificate, becoming the black and tan Ch. Zeus vom Schwarenberg. Madame Rikovsky had persuaded Herr Emil Schray to part with this yearling and he came to England making his debut at Cruft's in 1939, achieving his title before the onset of the Second World War. Zeus had made an outstanding contribution to the Smooth and Long stock, not only in England but, indeed, throughout the English-speaking section of the world.

Innumerable Champions are descended from this illustrious animal, the product of a vom Schwarenberg dam, who was sired by a Luitpoldsheim, and a sire of pure Luitpoldsheim stock. To mention them all would take too much space, the principal kennel to benefit being that of the Silvae prefix in the ownership of Mrs Grosvenor Workman. Zeus was mated in 1941 to a bitch carrying the Dachswald affix and in the ownership of Mrs Workman. From this mating came the famous Ch. Silvae Zebo, a dog possessing great bone, spring of rib and deep oval keel, who in turn sired a host of top flight Champions, not only for the Silvae kennel, but for many other breeders. In the litter with Zebo was a dog with a thick heavy coat, undoubtedly carrying the long-hair factor. He was sold to a pet home and lost sight of. Zebo, early in his stud career, sired Ch.s Lustre and Polish (Silvae) and a year later Ch. Silvae Banjo. Mrs Workman mated Banjo and Polish and from this union the outstanding dog Ch. Silvae Sailor's Quest was born. In only three years at stud, he became the sire of thirty Champions. Tragedy came his way early in life so this magnificent stud was lost. Australia benefited by the importation of his brother Silvae Querry, he doing for the Australian dogs what Quest had done for those in England.

Amongst Quest's Champion offspring was Mr Pilkington's dog Ch. Ashdown Skipper, a chocolate (Zebo's dam being this colour). Skipper's progeny won many Certificates between them, and eight became Champions. Madame Rikovsky's Ch. Urbatz von der Howitt, a black and tan, sired six Champions, amongst them Ch. Rhinefields Lenz.

Possibly Skipper's most famous son, a chocolate like himself, was Turlshill Pirate – a small dog and little shown, but nevertheless possessing great quality. He sired many Champions and became the grandsire of the famous Ch. Womack Wrightstarturn, winner of the 1967 Dachshund Club's Jackdaw Trophy for the Dog of the Year (any variety), and also of Australian Ch. Womack Wrightroyalshow. Wrightstarturn was retired from the show ring after Cruft's in 1970 having won thirty-eight Challenge Certificates.

The last of the Womacks (for Mrs Gale reduced her kennel after her husband's death) were Ch.s Womack Wrum Double and Wrum 'N' Coke. These are out of the last litter sired by Ch. Womack Wrightstarturn, who was twelve years old at the time of mating. Wrum Double sired three Champions, Ch. Womack Wrum Truffle and Ch. Teilwood Hot Toddy and Ch. Yatesbury Vanity Fair. The two Wrightstarturn offspring were ex Ch. Womack Wrum Bacardi, she by Ch. Eatina Sundowner ex Ch. Womack Wintermorn, thus doubling up on Ch. Wainwright. This kennel has bred twenty-five Champions in Smooths, with never more than ten adults at any time.

Ch. Womack Wrum Double by Ch. Womack Wrightstarturn ex Ch. Womack Wrum Bacardi. Owned and bred by Mrs Gale.

The success of the Womacks was the result of line breeding to the Quest son, Ch. Urbatz von der Howitt. Mr and Mrs Gale bought in Brockwood Rosy Future, daughter of Ch. Silvae Lustre (a son of Ch. Zebo), and a daughter of Groza von der Howitt, who in turn was a daughter of Ch. Urbatz. Rosy Future was mated to Ch. Urbatz. Groza's daughter Reanda Violetta was mated to Ch. Ardrahan Dorian, an Urbatz son ex Gazula von der Howitt, full sister to Groza von der Howitt. From these matings a dog was kept from one litter and a bitch from the second. These were eventually mated to produce Womack Wagonette, Wagonette for her first litter going to Ch. Aysdorn Black Zenith (grandson of Zebo); for her second, to Pirate. From this mating came Ch. Womack Wainwright. Zenith and Wagonette's offspring, Womack Winterbottom, became the sire of Womack Winterstar, who was the dam of Ch. Womack Wrightstarturn sired by Ch. Womack Wainwright.

The Gales bred seven English Champions in ten years, in addition to Champions in Australia, the Argentine and Canada. This breeding plan is of great interest in that it follows to completion my recommendation for the purchase of foundation stock as outlined in the chapter on founding a kennel. The Urbatz son in the ownership of the Gallops was Ch. Rhinefields Lenz. This kennel line bred to Ch. Urbatz, the Quest son, and in so doing founded the big winning strain. Ch. Lenz's most famous progeny were his grandchildren Ch.s Rhinefields Diplomat and his sister Dolabella, these two being by Ch. Silvae Virgo ex a Lenz granddaughter. Diplomat won the Jackdaw Trophy for 1968.

The Rhinefields continued to win top honours with a son of Ch. Diplomat – Ch. Rhinefields Dramatist. His dam, a Paxford bitch, was sired by Ch. Silvae Thackeray when mated to a daughter of Ch. Silvae Virgo. The next Champion dog from this home was Rhinefields Descendant by Ch. Dramatist. By Ch. Diplomat the Gallops made up Rhinefields Amapola – dam of Ch. Rhinefields Amala the breed's greatest winning bitch.

Ch. Dramatist sired good winning stock for several kennels. The Rosenkets used him as mate for their Ch. Swiss Miss combining Womack and Aravorny (again Rhinefields).

Ch. Rhinefields Amala by Ch. Descendant of Rhinefields ex Ch. Rhinefields Amapola. Owned and bred by Mr and Mrs J. Gallop (L. Mitchell).

The chocolate and tan colouring can be found in several kennels, the best known being the Turlshills of Mr Pinches. His principal sire, as previously stated, was Turlshill Pirate. The latter sired fifteen Champions, and out of this number, eight were chocolate and tan. His most famous near descendant is Ch. Turlshill Gay Lady, his granddaughter and the winner of thirty-three Challenge Certificates. Mr Pinches' original bitch, a daughter of Ch. Silvae Lustre, was Brookenville Blackbird.

From this line Mrs Rachel Hood-Wright bred a dog and bitch from the same litter by Pirate ex Turlshill Lorelei, the chocolate offspring of two parents with the same colouring. Mrs Hood-Wright made both these up to become Ch. Heidfeld Liesel and Ch. Heidfeld Lohengrin, who in turn sired two chocolate and tan Champions, Ch. Loni of Dunlewey and Ch. Helice of Hanstown.

Mr Pilkington's Ch. Ashdown Skipper, the chocolate son of Ch. Silvae Sailor's Quest, had to his credit four chocolate and tan Champions, including the famous Scottish bitch Ch. Dargarvel Mirth of Deugh.

In 1956 Mrs Hood-Wright of the Selwood prefix bred the red Ch. Selwood October Lad, who carried Quest no less than three times in the third generation. In 1957 she made up the chocolate and tan Selwood Scampari, again doubly bred to Quest, and in 1958 the chocolate and tan Ch. Sunsprite with Quest dominant.

In the year 1947, Mr Hague of the Limberins was coming to the fore, again with stock bred from Zeus. The Scottish kennels of Cedavoch, owned by Mr and Mrs McNaughton, were mainly founded on Turlshill, Aysdorn, Ashdown, Silvae, and Deugh. They constantly produce top winners for themselves, and, by use of their stud dogs, for others. To mention Cynosure of Cedavoch leads on to Ch. Cedavoch Sweet Cyn (who won many certificates and the Mariners Trophy of the Dachshund Club); Sweet Cyn's brother, Cedavoch the Swank of Ingerdorm, and her sister Ch. Auldrig Elan of Cedavoch were mated, and from this union came Ch. Cedavoch Modesty Forbids.

Miss Cook of the Deughs has had many top winners. To mention just two – Ch. Bart and Ch. Careless Rapture of Deugh – shows the strength of this kennel. These two are the parents of Plada of Deugh, who is the sire of Swank. Ashdown dogs and bitches appear frequently in the antecedents of her line.

Mr and Mrs Macaulay bred Timaru Trendy who, when mated to Alf Hague's Ch. Limberin Leading Light, became dam to the famous 'laughing litter'.

The Thundergays, in the ownership of Mr and Mrs Dalgetty, were well known for Ch. Thundergay Storm Cloud and Ch. Thundergay Double-O-Seven.

Unfortunately, with excessive transport costs and the long distances to be covered, we do not see very much of these good exhibitors. Those of us in the middle or south of the island are equally unwilling to make the long journey up north.

The Miniatures, both Long and Smooth, are in Scotland. The Smooths with Mrs Evans, Mrs Angus and Lady Dick Lauder; the Longs are owned by Mrs Pain (Candover) and Mrs Cole-Hamilton (Beltrim).

The foundation of the Limberins-Merryvale Marianna was a red daughter of Ch. Zick of Grunpark (Ch. Kunz Schneid appearing three times close behind him), ex Merryvale Julianna, a Ch. Zeus vom Schwarenberg daughter. Marianna went for her first mating back to Ch. Zeus and from this litter the black and tan Champion Lounge Lizard appeared, this dog being of interest to the long-haired variety in that, though he was a Smooth, he was carrying the recessive factor for long-haired coats, and himself sired six of this variety. The second mating of Marianna was to Ch. Silvae Sailor's Quest and Limberin Luxury Liner was retained, to be later mated to Silvae Dachscroft Bangard (a descendant of Ch. Zeus). Two bitches of outstanding quality were kept; the ancestor of all the Limberins (either Standard or Miniature), Limberin Lucy Locket being the most renowned.

In the late 1950s Mrs Foden of the Booth prefix and Miss Hill of Hawkstone imported from Belgium Heracles vom Liebestraum (von der Sauhatz breeding). This clear red dog proved to be dominant for his colour, medium in size and very sound. The best of the bitches used on him was one of Miss Hill's, Ch. Hawkstone Echo, the dam of Ch. Hawkstone Fusilier, a very good sire; before he died in Mrs Lawley's ownership, he left six Champion progeny. Ch. Echo was herself a daughter of Ch. Ashdown Eminent (Ch. Ashdown Skipper, Ch. Silvae Sailor's Quest). Mr Hague – Limberin – took advantage of this new blood-line and benefited enormously.

In 1973 he mated the dominant red Ch. Limberin Leading Light to a bitch, Timaru Trendy, which he had bought from Mr and Mrs Macaulay. She whelped Ch. Limberin Loud Laughter, Ch. Limberin

Ch. Limberin Loud Laughter by Ch. Limberin Leading Light ex Timaru Trendy. Owned and bred by Mr Alf Hague.

Low Laughter, and Ch. Limberin Light Laughter. The dog Loud Laughter went into the ring, winning his Certificate at seven months, and Best Puppy In Show at the Manchester Championship Show. Light Laughter, after winning his third Certificate, was sent to Australia, where he quickly added Australian Ch. to his title. Loud Laughter sired three champions.

Into the picture in 1969 came the kennel of Mr and Mrs Triefus, the Mithrils. Breeding had been continuous for some thirteen years and a bitch was in this year sent to the Champion son of Ch. Hawkestone Fusilier, Ch. Limberin Leading Light. The black and tan daughter of Ch. Silvae Virgo (line bred to Quest) produced five red puppies; it proved to be a most outstanding litter for similarity in construction, and of great soundness. All were multiple first prize winners at Championship shows by the time they had reached fifteen months; the dog had become a Champion, one bitch had won a Challenge Certificate, two others had reserve certificates and three were holders of the Junior Warrant and have since become Champions.

The writer (owner of the Imber prefix) had in 1960 sent a black and tan great granddaughter of Ch. Urbatz von der Howitt to Heracles vom Liebestraum, and from this complete outcross retained a red bitch, ultimately sending her to Ch. Womack Wainwright (the line-bred descendant of Ch. Urbatz). Two bitches from this litter became Champions. One, in the ownership of Mr and Mrs Gale, when mated to the famous Ch. Wainwright son, Ch. Womack Wrightstarturn, became the dam and grand dam of successive Womack champion stock. The other, the red Ch. Imber Auriga, was the ancestor of several Championship show winners, all very fixed for type.

For her last litter I mated Ch. Auriga to a dog I discovered when judging at the British Timken show in 1967. There was, in the classes, a red dog of great soundness and good type. I spoke to his owners, after judging, asking if I might use him, and how was he bred. His sire, Sidegate Hawkestone Forester, was a brother to Ch. Fusilier and so son to Heracles.

So much did I like Matzell Forrester, that I proposed that the Nortons should have pick of litter instead of a fee. And I realised that Marilyn (then I think thirteen years old) was very keen, already a good handler and ready to learn. In the resulting litter Imber Starshine and Imber Star Dream stood out. Star Dream became a Matzell, and with her this kennel was firmly established. Over the years they have consistently turned out a very correct type, latterly using the top Limberins, who were also descended from Heracles vom Liebestraum.

Take Heracles a stage further – Sqn Ldr and Mrs Henson come in with the Teilwoods. Some years back they acquired Rhodecot Autumn Leaves. This bitch, as Teilwood Rhodecot Autumn Leaves, had a litter to Starshine, Twilight being retained. Her next litter was to Ch. Womack Wrunning Flush, and this time Teilwood Autumn Ace was kept; the two, when mated, produced Teilwood Sadie.

Sadie, when mated, brought in the kennel of Mrs Heesom with the prefix Landmark, for Sadie was mated to Ch. Melchior. From this union two top flight bitches appeared. The Hensons keeping Red Delicious, making her up and winning B.O.B. at Cruft's in 1979. Mrs Heesom had purchased Rosie Lee, and with her did good winning. Chosen for her mating was Mrs Moore's Deepfurrows Romeo, a son of Mr Triefus's American import, Clarion Call von Westphalen. Their son made a spectacular start to his show career, becoming Ch. Landmark Sebastian at just over the year – he then became an Indian Ch.

Ch. Melchior, through his dam Ortrud of Landmark (double granddaughter of Ch. Turlshill Lancelot) is also sire to Ch. Landmark Magician with his dam Silvae Truffle.

Ch. Imber Veruschka, a black and tan granddaughter of Starshine and Imber Beechnut, takes the Womack and Imbers further along the line of the Ch. Zeus/Heracles mix.

For some years the descendants of Ch. Zeus had dominated the pedigrees of the big winners both at home and abroad. The introduction of the blood of the red Heracles tied up well with that of Zeus. At the end of 1970, a lovely red bitch, Silvae Jambo, was awarded the Best of Breed at Richmond Championship Show. She was a granddaughter of Sidegate Hawkstone Forester, a full brother to Ch. Hawkstone Fusilier, and being Silvae, had Quest in the background.

The Zeus stock over the years had great elegance combined with

Ch. Matzell Midas by Ch. Limberin Loud Laughter ex Matzell Miranda. Owned and bred by Mrs E. and Miss M. Norton.

Ch. Court Jester of Garelyn. By Ch. Benjamin of Ralines ex Larch of Dunlewey. Bred by Mrs J. Putsman. Owned by Mr & Mrs P. and Miss R. Lockett.

soundness, and invariably lovely heads. The heads on the reds had for long lacked this good feature but at last this was being remedied and the red Smooth Dachshunds were on a par with their black and tan relations.

The D'Ariscas of Mrs Coxon have made a big impact upon the Championship shows – one Champion following another. The foundation of this line, Urdac Electra, was purchased from Mrs Urwin for, in Mrs Coxon's words, 'the princely sum of 12 pounds'. She was mostly of Silvae and Eastmead breeding, and again in the owners's words, 'was of outstanding breed type, with classical head and superb outline. Her front was, however, not her fortune.' A breeding programme was planned, with priority being given to the choice of a dog with correct front and of as good breed type. For her first litter Cedavoch Sudden Calm of Gaybrook was used, bringing in a correct front. Of three dog puppies born, one was to become Ch. D'Arisca Satin Satan, winning the Certificate at Cruft's in 1969.

For her second litter, Electra went to Ch. Limberin Timaru Thunderbolt. A good bitch was retained, D'Arisca Satin Splendour. This one did reasonably well in the ring, and was then mated to Ch. Silvae Kennet. A daughter, Ch. D'Arisca Satin Sophisticate, went on to her title at twelve months old. From the latter's only litter, by Ch. Dargavel Most Happy Fella of Deugh, a dog was kept, and became Ch. D'Arisca

Satin Statesman, winning B.O.B. at Cruft's in 1976. Electra for her third litter went to Ch. Womack Wrightstarturn, this mating producing Ch. D'Arisca Satin Sensation. This bitch, when mated, produced Ch. D'Arisca Satin Selebration by Ch. Silvae Thackeray. Ch. Sensation was also mated to her half-brother Mormonstag Wallace, and produced the beautiful Ch. D'Arisca Satin Speculation, Ch. Selebration was mated to Ch. Statesman, from this came Ch. D'Arisca Status Symbol, another good winner at Championship Shows.

In 1978 Mrs Coxon decided to purchase an outcross bitch, and took, from Mr Pinches of the well-known chocolates, Turlshill Debutante. She made a sensational start to her show career, winning the very large Puppy Stakes class at the Great Joint Dachshund Championship Show, following this up by taking Best Bitch Puppy at Driffield Championship Show. Debutante is out of a litter by the Lockett's Ch. Court Jester of Garelyn, with his sire Ch. Benjamin of Ralines and her dam Lady Jane of Turlshill. On reading Lady Jane's pedigree, one notices that the chocolate and tan colouring is very much in evidence, Turlshill Pirate occurring four times. Turlshill Templar, her sire, is by Ch. Turlshill Highwayman, and she has this same dog in the bitch line. Debutante produced Ch. D'Arisca Adventurer when mated to a son of Status Symbol.

2 The Long-Haired Dachshund

The development of the Long Hair can be traced to the sixteenth century. In engravings of this period a Dachshund can be recognised with rather long hairs on the ears, a flag tail, and pronounced feathering on the flanks and the hinder side of the legs.

Research has found that this variety arose from the crossing of the Badger Digger with the old German Gun Dog (Wachtel or Stoberhund) by an unknown Forestry Official at the court of Johann Georg II of Anhalt Dessau (1660–65). Under Prince Leopold this variety was bred consistently, for their offspring proved to be great hunting dogs, easy to keep to heel. From these ancestors in the hunting kennels a strain of pure-bred black and tans was derived, these being regarded as valuable gifts in German Court circles. At that time they were described as having short legs, strong backs, profuse wavy coats and great courage. The coats in the course of years became neater and lighter. In the years 1799–1825, King Maximillian of Bavaria had as his favourite hunting dogs a pack of black and tans.

In 1868 a famous bitch Waldi aus dem Kaiserhaus was whelped. She came to be recognised as the tribal mother of the long-haired variety although she herself was descended from Smooth parents. Her breeder, a forester in the Tyrol, kept only Smooths, giving away any Long Hairs in his litters. From one of the descendants of Waldi there appeared at the end of the nineteenth century the first red long-haired Dachshund, the sire of this puppy being a Smooth red.

The history of the Long Hair in England begins with the importation in 1900 of stock from Austria. There were quite a number bred from this line and they found admirers in many private homes. Dr Fitch Daglish, later to become a great devotee of this variety, saw his first Long Hair whilst in Germany in 1908. He purchased a pair and began breeding. The outbreak of the 1914–18 war forced him to return to England and before doing so he distributed his stock amongst his German friends.

In 1922 the first of several imports arrived in this country, the dog being the red Ratzmann vom Habitschof from the kennel of Herr Hanks in South Germany, and the bitch German Champion Gretel III vom Lechtal. The dog had a glorious head, immense length, very heavy bone, sound close feet and a profuse coat of perfect texture. He was a big dog, but extremely active, with the carriage of an aristocrat. His fault when on the move was of closeness behind. He came out of quarantine in time to be entered for Cruft's in 1923. At that time there were no separate classes or breed registers for the different varieties of Dachshunds; Smooths had, up till then, been the only ones shown. Ratzmann was entered in the Open Class, which he duly won, carrying off the Certificate against the Smooth opposition.

This decision created something of a sensation, and should have gained friends for this handsome variety, but the exhibitors of the Smooths entered that day did not take their defeat kindly.

The bitch, Gretel, was also a very high-class specimen and difficult to fault. She had been imported as mate for Ratzmann, but unfortunately died before this could be accomplished. However, the importer of the pair re-visited Germany and bought a daughter of Ratzmann ex Gretel III. This bitch was a small black and tan of great quality and had had a successful show career in Germany before coming to England. She passed into the ownership of Dr Fitch Daglish and was mated to her sire producing many beautiful specimens. At that time there were no other stud dogs; consequently the progeny of this pair had to return to their sire or dam. The result of close inbreeding became very apparent, the mouths being badly overshot and loss of substance being very marked.

In 1928 the first of the 'von Fels' to enter England was imported, this being Elfe, in whelp to the German Grand Champion of that year, Stropp von der Windberg. The litter, born in quarantine, contained a dog and a bitch, she to become the first long-haired Champion as Ch. Rose of Armadale; the dog later to be Ch. Rufus of Armadale. Both these won their Certificates from Any Variety Dachshund competition.

Bred to existing stock, Ch. Rufus bred a long line of outstanding specimens, all possessing the heavy bone and perfect soundness for which he himself was renowned. His dam, Elfe von Fels and his sister Ch. Rose, were equally successful when mated to Ratzmann's son – Hengist of Armadale.

The famous von Walder kennel of Mrs Bellamy was founded on these lines; so too was the brilliantly successful kennel of Mrs Smith-Rewse, with the Primrosepatch prefix.

In 1930 the handsome dark-red Jesko von der Humboldshohe came to England. He was a medium sized dog who quickly became a Champion and a successful sire. In 1931 another 'von Fels', the exceptionally good dog Otter, was imported. He too quickly became a Champion. Mrs Bellamy was amongst the first to take advantage of the services of this bright light, using him to produce Ch. Karl von Walder ex a daughter of Elfe von Fels and his sister Ch. Micheline von Walder.

Ch. Karl sired, amongst other top flight dogs and bitches, Ch.

Magdalena von Walder, who when mated to Ch. Michael von Walder, a son of Ch. Rufus and Ch. Chloe of Armadale, bred Ch. Jack Horner von Walder and Ch. Miss Muffet von Walder in one litter. Jack Horner sired seven Champions, including three for the Hilltrees suffix of Colonel Hodge, two for the Northanger suffix of Mrs Howard Joyce and, in particular, Ch. Royce of Northanger, later to add to the history of the Long Hairs by siring Ch. Reanda Rheingold of Marlenwood. He was the sire of five Champions, two for the Kitenoras of Mrs Kidner, two for the Danjors of Mr Jordan, and one for the Mooncoins of Mrs Chatterton.

At a later date an in-whelp black and tan lightweight, combining the blood of von Fels and Habitschof, was imported as mate for Ch. Otter von Fels. The bitch whelped in quarantine and weighed only 13 lb. A dog from this mating who was registered as Knowlton Jochen weighed, at maturity, $17\frac{1}{2}$ lb, and for his size had excellent bone. His value as a stud was soon proved, Mrs Bellamy using him as sire on Ch. Micheline von Walder (Ch. Otter von Fels ex the Elfe von Fels daughter). Amongst the litter, the bitch Mona Lisa von Walder achieved fame when in the ownership of Mr John Pollard; he came into the variety in 1937. Mona Lisa was bred to Ch. Michael von Walder (Ch. Rufus of Armadale ex Ch. Chloe of Armadale) and produced the post-war (1939–45) Champion in Ch. Mira Erlenmark of Seton, the dam of Ch. and American Ch. Mauna Loa Erlenmark. Ch. Chloe was another daughter of Elfe von Fels by Hengist of Armadale, the Ratzmann von Habitschof son who had been the first long-haired import in the year 1922.

Knowlton Jochen had an equally famous sister in Knowlton Madel, who, when mated to Ch. Karl von Walder, produced, in her first litter, the outstanding Ch. Magdalena von Walder, who later whelped Ch. Jack Horner von Walder. In another litter to Ch. Karl von Walder she bred Jerica of Warstock, the brindle who in 1940 came into the ownership of Mr and Mrs Buck. They were already the owners of Jirfield of Warstock, also a brindle, and of Jacqueline of Warstock by Jumbo of Warstock, a son of Ch. Rufus of Armadale, ex Carmen of Stutton, a granddaughter of Ch. Otter and of Elfe von Fels. In 1938 Dr and Mrs Lea of the Warstock suffix bought the whole of the last litter by Ch. Karl von Walder ex Knowlton Madel, included in which were two brindle bitches, Jaglish and Jerica on which they founded the Warstocks. The Leas mated Jaglish to Ch. Otter, so producing the Bucks Jirfield of Warstock. Jirfield bred Ch. Ballerina of Buckmead who was a tiger-striped brindle and is the ancestor of all of the Buckmead stock. Jaglish, later, when in the possession of Mrs Howard Joyce and when mated to Ch. Jack Horner von Walder, whelped Ch. Royce of Northanger, the sire of Mrs Ireland-Blackburne's Ch. Robsvarl Jeneth of Marlenwood, Mrs Connell's Ch. Highlight von

Holzner and Mrs Gwyer's Ch. Reanda Rheingold of Marlenwood.

The Buckmeads can be found behind many well-known winners. Lady Kathleen Hare with the Reedscottage prefix had used an import, Kerlchen von der Godesburg, on Reedscottage Robina, and from this mating bred Ch. Reedscottage Rogueish, who was later mated to Ch. Jeremy of Buckmead (grandson of Ch. Buckmead Ballerina, the Jirfield of Warstock, Jacqueline of Warstock's daughter) and bred Ch. Reedscottage Rhythm, who produced Ch.s Buckmead Daemon and Dominic, mated to Ch. Buckmead Palomino. Another Buckmead appeared in a litter by the first Miniature long-haired Champion dog, Marcus of Mornyvarna ex Bacchante of Buckmead, she being Ch. Buckmead Miss Miniver. When she was mated to the Miniature Long Champion John of Mornyvarna, the sire of the future Ch. Buckmead Palomino was retained.

Mrs Chatterton of the Mooncoins, who had bred a Long Hair, Mooncoin Macushla by Ch. Reanda Rheingold of Marlenwood ex the Smooth Mooncoin Mona Lisa, mated her to Buckmead Sherry, the Ch. Jeremy of Buckmead's son.

The famous kennel of Standard Long Hairs and, later, Miniature variety, in the ownership of Mrs Smith-Rewse, under the suffix Primrosepatch, was founded on a typical brindle bitch, Bluebell of Armadale, daughter of Hengist of Armadale ex Elfe von Fels. She was later mated to Elfe's son, Ch. Rufus of Armadale, producing the first of the many Champions for this kennel – Ch. Golden Patch. When this bitch was mated to Ch. Otter von Fels, she whelped Ch. Roderick of Primrosepatch, and later Ch. Black Knight. The latter dog was sired by Krehwinkle of Primrosepatch, a son of Mrs Smith-Rewse's 1935 import, Alma von der Glom, who whelped in quarantine to the German Ch. Ebbo Krehwinkle.

Mrs Ireland-Blackburne of the Robsvarl prefix had her first bitch in 1935, a daughter of Ch. Rufus of Armadale, ex Bartonbury Velvet. Later she purchased, from Mrs Bellamy, Lisa von Walder, who was a daughter of Ch. Jaeger of Dilworth, himself a son of the 1930 import Jesko von der Humboldshohe. Her kennel bred six Champions and followed the Ch. Otter/Elfe von Fels line, through Ch. Jack Horner von Walder and the bitch, Jaglish of Warstock.

The Brincliffes of Miss Cheaney were prominent in the early 1940s and were founded on the bitch, Gretchen of Blenheimberry, by Knowlton Jochen (a son of the imports Blucher von der Drachenburg and Sola von Jungfrauental) ex a daughter of Ch. Karl von Walder and Ch. Chloe of Armadale. Gretchen, when mated to Ch. Michael von Walder, bred Margot of Brincliffe, who later was mated back to her great-grandsire Karl, and from this mating Ch. Nicholas of Brincliffe was whelped. He during his stud life sired five Champions, two for the

Hilltrees of Colonel Hodge and Ch. Robsvarl Ripple for Mrs Ireland-Blackburne. Gretchen, when mated to Ch. Jack Horner von Walder, whelped Ch. Christopher of Brincliffe, the sire of four Champions.

Following the war years 1939–45, Mrs Roberts with the Bolivar suffix was making great strides forward, breeding several Champions, both dogs and bitches. Possibly her greatest bitch was Ch. Jane of Bolivar, who was whelped in 1958 ex Ch. Griselda of Bolivar (Zip of Boliver ex Veronica of Bolivar). The sire of Ch. Jane (Ch. Imber Coffee Bean) was a long-haired descendant of the Smooth Ch. Zeus vom Schwarenberg.

During the years from the first of the imports in 1922 until the early 1950s, all breeding done by the leading kennels followed the same pattern, i.e. von Fels and Habitschof, for each and every kennel kept to the same lines. The lightweight Zola von Jungfrauental, dam of both Knowlton Madel and Knowlton Jochen, had von Habitschofs as both paternal and maternal granddams.

In 1954 Mr John Pollard, in an article on the Long Hair, stated that new blood was needed for this variety, and the way to obtain it was either by an import, or by using a recessive Long Hair. By this time the recessive factor carried by Ch. Zeus vom Schwarenberg was asserting itself. One of the first of the Smooths to produce the Long coats was a Zeus son, Ch. Limberin Lounge Lizard, whelped in 1948. He mated a Zeus daughter, Kelvindale Zest, and in the litter was the first of Miss Tilney's Long Hairs, Ch. Clonyard Corky. This was followed by the appearance of a black and tan Long Hair in a Smooth litter bred by Mrs Meyer, from Reanda Black Orchid, a daughter of Groza von der Howitt. Groza is of interest in that she was litter sister to Gazula von der Howitt and both were daughters of Ch. Urbatz von der Howitt, line bred to Ch. Zeus. Mrs Meyer's bitch soon became Ch. Reanda Satin Lassy and when mated to Ch. Royce of Northanger (Ch. Jack Horner von Walder's son) whelped the dog who became the well known Ch. Reanda Rheingold of Marlenwood, the sire of several Champions for the Danjors, the Kitenoras, and for Mrs Chatterton and Miss Tilney who later bred several Champions from her accidental entrance into the Long Hairs. Mrs Meyer had a second bitch (also a Smooth) to produce a Long Hair; this bitch, I think, was not bred from.

In 1950 a further infusion of the Long coat factor through two Smooth parents appeared in a litter by a son of Ch. Silvae Lustre (grandson of Zeus) ex Imber Gold Flake, five generations removed from the Long Hair Sari von Waldberg, a daughter of Bartonbury Viceroy, himself a son of Ch. Rufus of Armadale. In the litter were three Long coat and three Smooth coat puppies. The writer retained the three Longs. The bitches both died at an early age, but the dog was later registered as Imber Black Coffee and in his short show career won two Certificates. Mrs Connell, the owner of the von Holzners, had made up Ch. Highlight (son of Ch. Royce of Northanger by Ch. Jack Horner von Walder). He had mated a German import, Suse von Fuchensohl, who was a daughter of Erbs von Habitschof, so tying up with the earlier blood lines. The bitches had been retained by Mrs Connell and one became the property of the author's Imber Kennel as mate for Black Coffee. In the ensuing litter there was an outstanding red dog, who was later to make history in the long-haired variety, for, at his death thirteen years later, Imber Coffee Bean had sired fifteen Champions in England and others in Australia. He quickly achieved his title, and amongst the earliest of the breeders to take advantage of this new blood (through the Smooth Zeus line) was Miss Silcock, who had mated Rebecca of Spedding (daughter of Ch. Nicholas of Brincliffe) to him. From this mating Ch. Charlotte of Sarfra was retained, she being mated to Ch. Buckmead Daemon to produce Ch. Myfanwy of Sarfra, who was bred back to her grandsire, Ch. Imber Coffee Bean, and whelped the sisters Ch. Merula of Sarfra and Ch. Lerida of Sarfra.

Mrs Roberts of the Bolivar suffix sent Ch. Griselda of Bolivar (Zip ex Veronica of Boliver) to Coffee Bean. Ch. Jane of Bolivar, their daughter, became the dam of Ch. Kennhaven Mark and of Ch. Magda of Bolivar; these were sired by Ch. Buckmead Dominic (Ch. Buckmead Palomino ex Ch. Reedscottage Rhythm).

In 1955 Ch. Coffee Bean had been mated to his dam, Lisa von Holzner and from this mating Ch. Imber Café-au-Lait had been retained. He had also been mated to Wheyenna Peggotty (Ch. Jeremy ex Buckmead Maxine). From this litter the dog, Ch. Imber Café Noir, was kept, he later to sire Ch. Imber Café Tinto out of Imber Orangepip (Ch. Black Sambo von Holzner ex a Coffee Bean daughter, the full sister of Ch. Café-au-Lait).

Early in 1957 yet another line of recessive Long coats had appeared, this time through Imber Lancer, a Smooth red ex daughter of the red Ch. Grunwald Glade (Ch. Silvae Sailor's Quest ex Sally of Sunny-flowers, herself by Zick of Grunpark, a son of Ch. Kunz Schneid) and out of the dam of Imber Black Coffee, Imber Gold Flake. Mrs Jensen, of the now well-known Albaney Long Hairs, had mated a long-haired bitch to a Smooth grandson of Ch. Zeus; from this mating a smooth red bitch was kept. At a later date she was mated to Imber Lancer, and Ch. Zoe Celeste, a Long Hair of merit, was retained. The mating was repeated and this time another Long coat was kept to become the dam of five Champion progeny, three of them mated to Ch. Imber Café-au-Lait and the remaining litter sister and brother, by Coffee Bean. Possibly one of the best known of Mrs Jensen's winners was Ch. Rebecca Celeste of Albaney, the multiple Certificate winner, she being ex Anita and by Café-au-Lait (the inbred son of Coffee Bean).

Another sister to Anita, Deborah Celeste, when mated to Ch. Red Rebel of Albaney (Imber Cafecito ex Coffee Bean daughter), whelped

Ch. Rebecca Celeste of Albaney by Ch. Imber Cafe-au-Lait ex Anita Celeste of Albaney. Owned and bred by Mrs Jensen.

Ch. Red Simba of Albaney. From this dog Dr and Mrs Raven bred Ch. and Australian Ch. Kennhaven Diarmid and his sister, Ch. Kennhaven Danielli, they being line-bred to Ch. Buckmead Dominic on the dam's side.

Mrs Jensen, for her only litter, mated Rebecca Celeste to Ch. Coffee Bean, two dogs and a bitch breeding Champions. Mrs Martin bought Roberta Celeste, mating her to the Coffee Bean son, Dr and Mrs Raven's Ch. Kennhaven Caesar, one dog and bitch becoming Ch.s Mormonstag Rhoderick and Replica. The black and tan son of Rebecca, Ch. Murrumbidgee Black Titan of Albaney, was much used at stud and sired Mrs Rhodes's Ch. Coobeg Barbarossa; this dog was from a daughter of the American import, American Ch. Jessell's Sea Witch of Mountclown, line-bred to the 1939 export to the U.S.A. of Mrs Smith-Rewse's American Ch. Rose Brocade of Primrosepatch, a son of Krehwinkle of Primrosepatch, who was ex German import Alma von der Glonn. The red son of Rebecca, Imber Red Regent of Albaney, sired the big winning dog Ch. Red Rheingold of Albaney ex an Albaney bitch (sired by a Coffee Bean son Ch. Red Renegade, full brother to Ch. Oranje Celeste of Albaney).

Oranje Celeste was mated to Ch. Red Rheingold, Mrs Jensen making up Ch.s Camilla Celeste, Nicola Celeste and Nadine Celeste.

Camilla had three litters, each time to Imber Café Paulista, himself a grandson of Coffee Bean through his dam (bred by Mrs Jensen) Imber Samantha Celeste of Albaney, his sire being by an outcross dog of one hundred per cent German breeding. I had decided that an outcross was very necessary, and that I was the person to arrange this. I used an inbred Coffee Bean bitch hoping that in the third generation I should pick up the good points which I had come to expect.

Paulista died at ten years, having held the stud dog trophy for three years. He was succeeded by Ch. Swansford Brigg of Truanbru, then by his son Ch. Albaney's Red Rheinhart, ex Ch. Camilla Celeste of Albaney, who for three years won the Ch. Imber Coffee Bean stud award. His sons include Ch. Phaeland Phreeranger, Ch. Phaeland Chablis, Ch. Africandawns Wagonmaster, and Ch. Imber Hot Coffee. Ch. Phreeranger is sire to Ch. Jamanean Charlotte Ann whose brother, Jamanean Royal Celebration is a big winner and sire of the Best Puppy in show at the Long Hair Club's 50th Championship Show, Ch. Phasionman.

Ch. Phaeland Phreeranger by Ch. Albaney's Red Rhinehart ex Silksworth Gold Braid. Owned and bred by Miss S. Gatheral.

From the other two matings of Camilla to Paulista, the progeny became Ch.s Clare and Miranda Celeste, with Charm Celeste winning a ticket.

Other Champions by Paulista are ex daughter of Imber Red Regent of Albaney and Imber Kaffa Moka (Imber Café Brasileno of Voryn); Ch. Jamanean Maria is in the ownership of Mr and Mrs Robinson who at that time were novices. Also, Tony Johnson of the Africandawns made up his first Champion – Murrumbidgee Paganini – with the dam Ch. Pandora of Murrumbidgee.

Africandawns Night Banner, a Paganini son, has two Champion daughters in the Swansford prefix.

The Imbers came back into the picture through Coffee Bean's daughter, Samantha Celeste, and her son Paulista. For Kaffa Moka's second litter I decided to take her to Ch. Red Rheinhart, and from this union bred Ch. Imber Hot Coffee, who was the winner of three Hound

Groups and the sire of Australian Champion Irish Coffee with eight Champions here.

Ch. Nadine Celeste had just one litter, that to the litter brother of Ch. Imber Café Russe of Voryn (double Coffee Bean).

Mrs Lloyd Williams had bought from Mrs Jensen in 1962, the bitch Ch. Shula Celeste of Albaney (Ch. Imber Café-au-Lait ex Anita Celeste of Albaney) and with her made the Lynocree prefix well known. For her only mating, that to Ch. Kennhaven Mark of Bolivar, she whelped two dogs to achieve fame as Ch.s Lynocree Sabre and Solero.

From Mrs Jensen I purchased Albaney's Mia Celeste, eventually mating her to Hot Coffee and sending one of the offspring, Imber Irish Coffee, to Mrs Berge Phillips in Sydney, where, in her ownership, he added Australian Champion to his name.

Ch. Imber Hot Coffee by Ch. Albaney's Red Rhinehart ex Imber Kaffa Moka. Owned by Miss Raine and Mr Crawford. Bred by Miss Raine.

Imber Samantha Celeste was mated for her first litter to Imber Red Regent of Albaney (thus a double Coffee Bean litter was whelped). From this litter I gave Jeff Crawford a bitch to become his first Champion as Imber Café Russe of Voryn. She was mated to Mr and Mrs Paul Johnson's Rudolf of Langton Paddock, he carrying on the dam's side the American blood-line imported by Mr Emanuel, combined with that of Pipersbath. Rudolf's sire, Black Rock of Voryn, is also the grand sire of Kaffa Moka, who is a daughter of Samantha Celeste. Ch. Café Russe whelped only four puppies; the bitch pup was purchased by Mr and Mrs Robinson, they made her up as their second Champion, registered Voryn's Volga Olga. Ch. Phaeland Phreeranger was chosen as the sire for Olga's litter. Miss Susan Gatheral took a dog from the litter, and he quickly won his Junior Warrant as Jamanean Royal Celebration. Mr and Mrs Robinson made up Ch. Jamanean Charlotte Anne and Mrs Phillips made up Aus. Ch. Jamanean Maxie.

Mr and Mrs Bishop with Africandawns Erotic Touch (Paganini) own a small but select kennel, to which they added, in 1977, the black and tan Baron Zucker Kaiser of American breeding. Tony Johnson took to this dog, a descendant of Paulista (double granddaughter), and in her litter came Ch. Africandawns Yank-Go-Home. With Coffee Bean in so many present-day pedigrees, Zucker may provide the outcross that is so badly needed – time will tell.

In the late 1950s Mr Barton Emanuel took up residence in England with his kennel of Long Hairs of mainly American breeding, and with the early ancestors from the Primrosepatch kennels. Ch. Jinglebells Jocular of Mountclown, being used for Maybelle of Mountclown, bred Rossweise of Mountclown, and Mrs Connell used him as mate for Ch. Marina von Holzner, breeding Ch. Jacqueline von Holzner and combining Ch.s Highlight von Holzner and Nicholas of Brincliffe. Mrs Rhodes mated Reedscottage Roguish Wink, granddaughter of the German import Kerlchen von der Godesburg, to the American Ch. Jaeger of Barcedor and bred Ch. Coobeg Long Jonathan.

Dr and Mrs Raven had sent to Ch. Imber Coffee Bean the bitch Kennhaven Wendy, a daughter of Ch. Buckmead Dominic and Ch. Charlotte of Kitenora, herself a daughter of Ch. Reanda Rheingold of Marlenwood (Ch. Royce of Northanger ex Ch. Reanda Satin Lassy) and from this litter had kept a black and tan dog who was later to become Ch. Kennhaven Caesar. This great dog won over forty Certificates and sired eight Champions.

In 1963 Mr and Mrs Spiers of the Murrumbidgee suffix had purchased a bitch puppy from Miss Silcock; she was to become Ch. Merula of Sarfra. She combined the blood of the Buckmeads and the Imbers, and when mated to the litter brother of Ch. Pandora of Murrumbidgee (Pimpernel) whelped three bitches. One of these bitches became Ch. Endora of Murrumbidgee in the ownership of Mr and Mrs Swann.

Endora, for her first litter, went to Ch. Kennhaven Caesar. Her son and daughter won their titles as Ch. Swansford Ambassador and Adora. For the second litter she was mated with a black and tan bred by Mr and Mrs Cunningham – Brigg of Truanbru. The Swanns, having purchased this dog, added their prefix and showed him to his Championship. His sire was Ch. Murrumbidgee Black Titan of Albaney, and his dam Ch. Kennhaven Francesca.

Ch. Brigg became a very big winner with multiple Certificates, five Hound Groups and Reserve Best in Show at Edinburgh. From the mating with Endora two went to the top – Ch.s Swansford Estee and Eminence.

Ch. Endora, mated again to Brigg, whelped Ch. Swansford Toreador, yet another big winner and now sire of Ch. Swansford Waldeman.

Ch. Adora mated to Ch. Mooncoin Maccabean bred Mrs Whinchurch's Ch. Swansford Shenondor. Mated twice to Africandawns Night Banner (Ch. Paganini), Ch. Estee has two Champion daughters; one is Mrs Swann's Betadora and the other Mrs Whinchurch's Ch. Swansford Odora from Brianolf.

Ch. Swansford Zsazadora by Ch. Skywalker Self Raising Sid ex Swansford Kistadora. Owned and bred by Mrs M. Swann.

A second bitch from Mrs Spiers to the Swanns won her title as Swansford Murrumbidgee Isadora (Dante of Murrumbidgee ex Ch Pandora, Dante being a son of Ch. Black Titan). Isadora had a litter by Ch. Imber Hot Coffee and their daughter Liesl became a Champion. Liesl had three litters to Ch. Toreador producing three champions.

Mrs Swann and Mrs Dixon, in partnership, own Ch. Frankanwen Gold Spinner of Swansford by Shenondor ex Frankanwen Golden Girl.

Another kennel to do well with a son of Ch. Brigg is that of Mr and Mrs Hall. Ch. Bronia Zodiac was bred by Mrs Hanney, his dam was Phaeland Juniper by Phaeland Saffron, a son of Ch. Red Renegade of Albaney ex Ch. Clonyard Casserole. Casserole was closely descended from the recessive Long Hair line carried by Ch. Limberin Lounge Lizard and Kelvindale Zest (Ch. Zeus).

Mr and Mrs Cunningham had kept Ch. Brigg's sister, mating her to Ch. Mormonstag Cannylad by Ch. Kennhaven Caesar ex Roberta Celeste of Albaney (double Coffee Bean). From this mating Tony Johnson bought in Truanbru Beau Brummel, who, with Africandawns added to his name, went on to become a Champion. The Cunninghams made up his sister as Ch. Truanbru Bunbury Blossom.

The Rosenkets of Mr and Mrs Rawson had, as their foundation bitch, Ritterburg Rhine Romantica, who was double granddaughter of Ch. Lynocree Sabre by Kennhaven Mark of Bolivar ex Ch. Shula Celeste of Albaney. She has had two litters to Hot Coffee and one to Imber Café Paulista. In the first litter was Ch. Rosenket Royal Flame; in the second and third litters were Royal Icing and Royal Kestrel, both well-known winners.

To sum up, the blood of the vom Schwarenberg–Luitpoldsheim mating, as combined in the Smooth Ch. Zeus vom Schwarenberg, had brought to the Long Hairs a much-needed outcross, through the recessive factor carried by this dog. The German Teckel Klub was founded in 1889 and long before that date certain strains occasionally produced the odd Long coat in a smooth-bred litter. I have referred to the famous bitch, whelped in 1868 from a Smooth litter, who became the ancestor of the red Long Hairs. Her breeder, a forester in the Tyrol, keeping only Smooths, giving away any Long Hairs which appeared in these litters. In my opening paragraphs I have mentioned the black and tans great hunting ability in their native Austria. Zeus brought to the Smooth Hairs great soundness and elegance; this he has also bequeathed in no small measure to his long-haired descendants.

PEDIGREE OF CH. ZEUS VOM SCHWARENBERG

German Teckel Stud Book No. 371197 K.
Born 9 March 1937.
Breeder: Herr Emil Schray, Stuttgart-Ditzingen, Romerhof 9.
From an article by Anneliese Wurm, Germany

'Breeders of smooth-haired Dachshunds are often surprised when long-haired puppies occasionally occur in litters from Smooth parents, especially when, on checking back the pedigrees of both parents, no Long Hair can be found among the ancestors.

'This has happened in litters going back to the well-known Smooth stud dog "Zeus vom Schwarenberg" who was imported into England in 1939.

'Asked to find out how far back the long-haired ancestors can be found in the pedigree of Zeus I anticipated no difficulties in following the lines in the German Stud Books.

'However, in spite of searching the stud books back beyond the turn of the century to 1889 nothing appeared to offer a clue. Until 1924 long-haired puppies in otherwise Smooth litters had been registered as of the Long variety with the note "Kurzhaarblut" (smooth blood-lines). After that date the crossing of Smooth and Long coats was forbidden and no litter of Smooth parentage containing long-haired puppies could be entered in the stud book even if it could be proved that no "false" mating had occurred, so that the appearance of long-haired puppies in what should be a smooth litter is something of which our breeders are much afraid.

'I discussed the whole matter with Herr Schray, the owner of the "Schwarenberg" affix. He, having been a breeder for more than forty years, had found it always to be a pity when after 1924 these Long Hairs could not be used by Long Hair breeders because these very specimens turned out to be excellent in every respect. He himself never kept any Long Hairs and never did any coat crossing at all, his only interest always having been the Smooths. Until 1924 nobody was bothered by these "outcrosses" and did not ask where they were coming from. Herr Schray drew my attention to some facts which will explain what can happen even now; unexpected Long Hairs in Smooth litters.

'Before the turn of the century Dachshunds of pure breed were sometimes not entered in the stud book because of the laziness or lack of knowledge of their owners, often foresters or hunters and not very interested in such paper work.

'These dogs could be judged by three judges *auf Begutachtung* (on appearance) and their progeny later be entered in the stud book with the remark "parent's pedigree unknown"). This, however, was only permitted in the early days of Dachshund breeding and was given up after the First World War. Today *no* Dachshund will be entered without at least three generations of pure and registered ancestors. The genetical construction of those Teckels could not be fully checked and, this may be one reason for not knowing when the first mixing of coats happened. The breeders of that time – not as numerous as they are today – very soon noticed that certain studs mated to certain bitches got puppies of both coats.

'I found the book *Der Dachshund* written by Herr Dr (Med) Engelmann (the so-called Dachshund breeders' bible), to be a very authentic source. Published in 1923 and for more than twenty-five years out of print, a new edition has now appeared. Herr Dr Engelmann not only hunted and bred all varieties of Dachshunds and judged at shows and field trials but was the greatest personality amongst the German Dachshund folk. He died in 1935 at the age of sixty-one but his book remains of great value to the present day.

'I should like to give his personal opinion on the matter of crossing Smooth and Long Hair, and in the following give a translation of the pages dealing with that question:

"Many breeders will know the excellent Long-haired Dachshund Schlupp-Saarau who was outstanding in coat, colour and construction, many times Best of Breed at important shows and for many years at the top of the long-haired variety. His pedigree goes back to excellent and outstanding ancestors, many of them champions and all of clear red colour – showing that all of them were smooth-haired! One of his brothers, Lump-Saarau, was a Long Hair too.

"In litters checked back to Hundesports Waldmann, 37, Long Hairs were born 'by accident' and nobody was able to say where they were coming from.

"I also remember Waldmann vom Tal and Waldine du Nord who in spite of being Smooth had Long-haired puppies, which many breeders explained by the relationship of these Dachshunds to the 'Flott-Sonnenberg, 668' line. Every breeder must realise that in spite of really pure breeding in coat he must expect throwbacks to old 'outcrosses' in coat. The same thing happens with features now long forgotten such as white paws, legs half white, white spots or patches on forehead or chest, which are found in the breed of the Dachsbracken even today...."

In his section dealing with the Mendelian Laws of Heredity, Dr Engelmann writes:

'When crossing Smooth and Long Hair, the Smooth proves to be dominant unless it happens to have long-haired ancestors. When both parents are pure bred the Long Hair disappears in the first filial generation:

1st Parental generation: Pure Smooth × Pure Long SS (homozygous LL (homozygous).

1st Filial generation: S1 × S1 (heterozygous) Smooth carrying Long factor.

2nd Filial generation: SS, S1, S1, LL.

SS and LL (homozygous) will always breed true.

S1 will breed in the way of the F2 generation, being heterozygous, that is Smooth with latent Long Hair.

'It is important for the breeder to realise that Long Hairs mated together will always produce Long Hairs in spite of having Smooth ancestry. Without doubt the Long Hair breeder can use these Long Hair puppies out of Smooth litters for breeding purposes, for usually no throwback to smooth coat will occur, only one case having come to my knowledge. On the other hand no breeder of Smooth can be sure of not getting Long Hair puppies, because all Teckels going back to Waldmann vom Tal, 449 line or the Flott-Sonnenberg, 668 line have proved to carry the latent Long Hair factor.'

These remarks by Dr Engelmann should provide us with the clue to the pedigree of Zeus.

One of the most outstanding ancestors of Zeus was the Smooth black and tan dog von Spree-Athen, 11216, Born 12 May 1910. He had a high record of show wins and would be called a Champion today. He was a widely used stud dog who appears on the Zeus pedigree:

In 8th generation – 27 times
In 7th generation – 8 times
In 6th generation – 1 time

On the dam's side Tenor's pedigree could be traced to Flott-Sonnenberg, 668, born on 25 June, 1889, appearing in the 5th, 6th and 7th generation.

On the sire's side Tenor goes back to Hundesports Waldmann, 37, appearing in the 7th generation.

Both these Smooth ancestors are the Dachshunds mentioned by Dr Engelmann as being known to have long-haired progeny. It is probably from these dogs that the lines can be followed, along which the recessive gene for Long Hair has been transmitted.

Of course, we cannot say that *all* their offspring have been heterozygous Smooths (S1 – Smooth carrying the gene for Long Hair) as some of the offspring must have been homozygous Smooth (SS), playing no part in the transmission of the Long Hair gene since they do not carry it at all.

In addition to Tenor, a well-known bitch played an important part in the construction of Zeus vom Schwarenberg's pedigree. This was Loni, 12127, bred by Herr Sensenbrenner who later took the affix vom Luitpoldsheim. In the 7th generation of Zeus, Loni appears six times – each time mated to Tenor. Loni herself in the 7th generation on her sire's side goes back to Hundesports Waldmann.

In the 8th generation of Zeus the mating of Loni to Tenor actually occurs eleven times! The result of that mating, the bitch Traudl vom Luitpoldsheim 13505K, appears as a combination of blood lines going back to Flott-Sonnenberg, 668, and Hundesports Waldmann, 37, as well. There should be no doubt that Traudl vom Luitpoldsheim must have been a heterozygous Smooth transmitting the gene for Long Hair to her descendants.

To bring out the Long Hair coat *both* parents have to be heterozygous Smooths. Traudl appears on the sire's side of Zeus as well as on his dam's side and we can suppose this to have played an important part in the genetical construction of Zeus and his progeny.

Another daughter of Tenor was Frigga vom Lindenbuhl, 12659K, whose son Illo vom Lindenbule, 4869K (strongly inbred to his grand-sire Tenor), also appears on both sides of the Zeus pedigree – eleven times in the 7th generation and twice in the 6th – and is also probably responsible for Zeus being a heterozygous Smooth (S1).

During the war the importation of dogs into England was impossible. Owing to this and to his excellent qualities and influence as a stud dog Zeus vom Schwarenberg played an important part in the construction of the English Smooth Dachshund. The 1957 Champions listed in the Dachshund Club Handbook are nearly all progeny of Zeus. No wonder that many of them may be heterozygous Smooths which mated together can produce long-haired puppies. Every litter of which both parents are Smooth and both descended from Zeus can be regarded as a 'test mating', and if long-haired puppies result then both parents are proved to be heterozygous Smooths (S1).

3 The Wire-Haired Dachshund

The Wire-haired Dachshund is derived from the crossing of the Smooth Teckel with the Dandie Dinmont and the Miniature wire-haired Pinscher – the Schnauzer. The early breeders succeeded in endowing the Dachshund with tremendous boldness and courage inherited from the Terrier and the Pinscher, and with the greatly improved coat of the Schnauzer. The earliest mention of this rough-coated Dachshund appears in 1797 and again in 1812 when Dr Walther refers to the excellent work done by these dogs.

One of the first to breed a good rough-haired Dachshund was Captain von Wardenburgh: he showed his dog Mordax at the Berlin show in 1888. This dog had a good outline but a soft coat. The breed has sprung from the mating of the Smooth with the Pinscher and it was due to this that in the beginning there often appeared a throw-back to the rough-haired Pinscher, this being shown by the head of the dog being too short and too small. In 1889 at the International Show held at Kassel, the Chief Forester, Herr Hesse, showed a whole collection of rough-haired Dachshunds, which, with the exception of two or three, still showed a great deal of Pinscher type. All had, however, a very rough coat of incomparable colour, the real colour of a wild cat, i.e. a proper combination of pepper and salt.

At the formation of the Teckel Klub in 1888 a mere three Wire Hairs had been registered; sixty years later this figure had risen to over two thousand for that year.

By 1948 Dr Schneider Leyer stated that the Wire-haired, while still possessing an excellent coat, showed an inheritance of less satisfactory characteristics such as the soft Dandie topknot, the Pinscher type head and the straight shoulders of the Schnauzer. He found that the breeding of this variety of coat was quite the most difficult and that the best of the Wires had gone to Sweden. In that country the German judges were full of admiration for the excellence of the stock. This was credited to the environment, the fish diet and to the skill of the Swedish breeders. The introduction of the Dandie blood was brought about, according to Dr Ilgner, by the horse traders from Mecklenburg returning home with a Dandie Dinmont.

The first Wire to be introduced to England was the dog Woolsack bred in 1888 and imported by a breeder of Smooths. From his photograph the dog appears large with very exaggerated hind-quarters. No progress was made with this variety until 1927, when in that year the Wire-haired Dachshund Club was formed, the President being Air Vice-Marshal Sir Charles Lambe K.C.B. All the founder members of the Club were experienced breeders in other breeds and fully realised the need for importing only the best available stock. The policy was quickly rewarded, for when these Wires made their show debut they were very well received. Classes for Wires were introduced in 1927, whilst at Cruft's in 1928, Lady Berwick, who had imported several from Czechoslovakia prior to 1927, won the Open Class.

Amongst the first imports, Mrs Howard of the Seale suffix bought Moritzel von der Abtscheck, to act as founder of her kennels, but unfortunately he died before siring a puppy.

Mrs Blandy was one of the pre-Second-World-War prominent exhibitors. She owned Anna of Nunneshall, daughter of the imported Daisy von Fichtenhain of Nunneshall, who had come over in-whelp to Puck von Aberbruck, and from her bred the lovely Ch. Achsel in 1929. Anna had been mated to the son of the imported Brita of Tavistone who had come to England mated to Wicht St Georg. Miss Theo Watts of the Tynewydds had bought him as a puppy. Major Emil Ilgner, the German authority on the Dachshund and in particular the Wire, under the kennel name of Erdmannsheim, came to judge at the Great Joint Dachshund Championship Show in 1932 and awarded Ch. Achsel first in a class of sixteen in Open Dog. Achsel sired many outstanding winners, with Champions in England and others, who, when exported to America to the ownership of Mr Frelingheysen, quickly established a winning line.

Mrs Blandy bred also from Anna of Nunneshall, Ch. Anetta, a red bitch of great quality. She had imported Distel von Konigshufer and mated her to Ch. Achsel, breeding Ch. Amelia, an excellent little dog.

Air Vice-Marshal Sir Charles Lambe, the owner of the famous suffix Dunkerque was a leading figure in the breed from 1927 until his death twenty-five years later. His first bitch was a present, and she became the foundation of the line through her son Michael of Dunkerque. Around 1934 Sir Charles felt that new blood was needed, so together with Miss Watts, Mrs MacCaw and Mr Stanhope Joel imported from Sweden the small, very sound dog Sports Mentor II. He proved of great value to the breed, siring two Champions.

In 1937 the well-known breeder Miss Seton Buckley also imported from Sweden that sensational bitch Wizden Sports Primavera of Seton. She had a brilliant show career and was the first of her breed to become an International Champion. She came to England in-whelp to Sports Troll and her litter included an excellent black and tan dog Petrouchka of Seton, who excelled in front, shoulder placement and back-line. In 1939, Miss Seton Buckley imported a dog, Theatre Street of Seton, ex the litter sister of Primavera, the Swedish Ch. Sports Spielerin.

In 1931 Mrs Howard (Seale) had acquired on the death of the owner of the Tavistones, three bitches and a dog, in partnership with Lady Schuster, these doing much to lay the foundation of the Seale suffix. Another Tavistone passed into Mrs Howard's ownership and proved a most valuable brood.

The war years inflicted a grave setback to the Wire-haired variety. Many of the older breeders had disposed of all their stock and were unable, either through age, or for personal reasons, to restart their kennels. The great majority of the pre-war winners were either too old or dead. Only Miss Seton Buckley and Mrs Howard had kennels of any size remaining, and their stock were almost the only representatives of the variety to be seen when shows started up again.

Miss S. N. Evans did much for the variety in that she mated her Wire bitch Trix of Dunkerque, a daughter of Sports Mentor II, to a Smooth son of Ch. Firs Black Sheen (grandson of Ch. Wolf von Birkenschloss), breeding the outstanding Champions Wylde Enchanter and Encore. Enchanter was mated to Ch. Midas of Seton, whose sire I.K.C. Paganini of Seton, was by Petrouchka of Seton, and son of the imported Sports Silence of Seton. Her litter included Ch. Wylde Cantata and Wylde Canoodle. Mercury of Seton, litter brother to Ch. Midas, mated to Enchanter, produced Ch. Wylde Surmise. Ch. Wylde Cantata later went to the U.S.A. and joined the kennel of Mrs Westphal and became the grandsire of the famous Vantbe's Draht Timothy, a multiple group winner. Miss Evans did great service to the Wire-haired Dachshund and deserves much credit for rescuing them from near obliteration following the war years. She bred eight Champions and was instrumental in selling foundation stock to several enthusiasts, amongst these being the Moat Kennel of Mrs Rice-Evans and Miss Dodds. Their original stock was descended from the mating of Ch. Wylde Encore to Retann Courante, a daughter of Ch Wylde Caprice. From this mating was bred Ch. Moat Leprechaun, who when mated to Vega of Clouds (Hobel aus dem Lohegau, imported), bred Ch. Jonquil of the Moat. The latter's daughter, when mated to Clouds Elinda Terceiro, whelped the foundation bitches of Miss Joan Hughes' Meeching kennels and of Mrs Amy Wilson, these being Rytona Twinkle and Tip Toe. Both became Champions. Twinkle visited the famous Ch. Gisbourne Inca, grandson of Ch. Coq D'or of Seton, the great-grandson of the imported Sports Silence of Seton. Miss Hughes has only a small kennel, continually breeding show stock of the highest class. From the mating of Ch. Twinkle to Ch. Inca, a dog and bitch became Champions, the bitch Tosca returning to her sire for a litter.

From this, a really lovely bitch was kept, Tessa of Meeching. After winning two Certificates she unfortunately died whilst whelping.

Ch. Tosca, however, visited Ch. Mordax Music Master and produced Ch. Tina and Trilby and Turandot (both have three Reserve Certificates). Turandot was mated back to Music Master and from this litter Toscanini was kept, and Tabitha was shown by the Latters. Trilby was mated to Ch. Gisbourne Milton and two winning bitches from this litter are Twinkle (kept) and Tassoula. Trilby has since mated twice to Ch. Joydonia French Mustard. From the first of these litters one dog became Ch. Oneva Tarragon of Meeching in the ownership of Mr & Mrs Bright as did Ch. Meeching Topsy Turvy of Oneva from the second litter.

In 1951 Mrs Bettie Farrand, with the Mordax prefix, who had previously shown Smooth Hairs, turned to the Wire-haired variety with Grunwald Graduate and Gracious, the dog soon becoming a Champion.

In 1956 she was showing a dog and bitch, both becoming Champions, Ch. Coral of Seton and her litter brother Ch. Coq D'or of Seton. These combined the blood of the Sports imports, through Ch. Midas of Seton, the grandson of Petrouchka of Seton son of the Swedish Sports Silence, which can be traced back on both sides of the pedigree. This pair were chocolate in colour. The sire of these, Ch. Grunwald Graduate, having been bred by Mr and Mrs Lloyd from Ch. Gerhardt of Wytchend (Ch. Midas of Seton) ex Twinkletoes of Seale by Ch. Jack Tar of Erlegh (Sports Mentor II), appears three times in the third generation behind the big winning Ch. Inca, his dam being a daughter of Ch. Coq D'or. Inca made history in the show world, having won

Ch. Gisbourne Inca by Ch. Gisbourne Indigo ex Gisbourne Camilla. Owned by Mrs Farrand. Bred by Mrs Quick.

fifty-six Challenge Certificates, with many Best in Show awards to his credit, five of them at Championship Shows, for the year 1964 he was awarded Dog of the Year. Inca is the sire of many Champions. His breeder Mrs Quick has a splendid type of Wires and is a consistent winner.

Amongst Inca's Champion offspring we have Ch. Mordax Music Master ex Brockbane Rachel; this dog has given the variety excellent construction of body. Amongst his Champion progeny we have Ch. Andyc Moonlight Rhapsody, Ch. Brockbane Red Rondo, Ch Pickhill Golden Minstrel, Ch. Tan Trudie of Thornton and Ch. Meeching Tina. Ch. Red Rondo has sired Ch. Daxglade Dancing Major of Swansford, with his sister the dam of Ch. Quitrutec Friendly Persuasion. Ch. Dancing Major is sire of Ch. Daxene Yukonly and Mrs Workman's Ch. Silvae Cotillion.

Ch. Andyc Moonlight Rhapsody by Ch. Mordax Music Master ex Moonmist of Andyc. Owned and bred by Miss Raphael.

Counted amongst Ch. Golden Minstrel's progeny is Ch. Fraserwood Neon Star ex D'Arisca Tweed and Tawny, a daughter of Irish Ch. Revolution of Seton. Minstrel during his show career won many certificates and Hound Groups with reserve B.I.S. at Leicester in 1977.

Mrs Farrand has the knack of selecting young puppies from bitches brought to her dogs, bringing them on, training them for the ring, and entering them with the youngster mature and ready to go to the top. The latest in the kennel is Ch. Krystona Augustus ex Pickhill Poinsettia (sister to Golden Minstrel), sired by Vagabond of Gisbourne.

Miss Raphael of the Andycs owns another very consistent Northern kennel.

A successful newer exhibitor, Mrs Milden, has recently made up Ch. Joydonia French Mustard, a son of Ch. Red Rondo.

Ch. Krystona Augustus by Vagabond of Gisbourne ex Pickhill Poinsettia. Bred by Mrs D. Atterton. Owned by Mrs B. Farrand and Mrs J. Naylor.

Mrs Flynn of the Culdees kennels owned the litter sister to Ch. Twinkle and Ch. Tip Toe, Rytona Tinsel; this bitch, being mated to a son of Ch. Moat Leprechaun, bred Ch. Culdees Katinka. Mrs Flynn, in partnership with Miss Hill of the Hawkstone Smooths, had for some while been breeding for the dapple colouration in the standard Wires. This had been achieved through mating a dominant Wire dog, Culdees Konz (brother to Ch. Katinka), to a silver dapple Smooth of Miss Hill's. In this litter amongst the whelps were two brindle dapple bitches. The next step was in mating Konz to one of his daughters. This time the whole litter were brindle dapples. From this mating, a dark brindle dog Hawkstone Osprey was kept, he being mated to Culdees Tapestry, a dark brindle descended from the black and tan Ch. Altair of Clouds bred in the 1950s from the import Hobel aus dem Lohegau. A black and tan dog was retained, and later mated to his grandmother; one of those from the first litter, Konz, was mated to the Smooth dapple bitch, and in this litter were two silver dapples. Konz has a Champion daughter to his credit, Ch. Lydia of Haverburg.

Mrs Gower had her first Champion in the early 1960s, the bitch Ch. Mordax Miss Mint having been bred by Mrs Farrand, ex a bitch by Ch. Grunwald Graduate, and by Grunwald Grampion, a son of Checkmate of Seton, ex the imported Sports Choreatium of Seton. Grampion's dam, Twinkletoes of Seale, was also the dam of Ch. Grunwald Graduate. In 1969 Mrs Gower made up her first home-bred Champion, a bitch by Moat Imperial, Ch. Amphletts Imperial Star.

Mrs Hoxey-Harris was a keen exhibitor for many years, turning out an excellent type. Her first Champion, Tumlow Truffle, was by Retann Barley Sugar, bred from the mating of a Dunkerque-Seale bred bitch, Demerara of Doms. Tumlow Toffee mated to Moat Fame (Ch. Moat Leprechaun-Vega of Clouds sister to Ch. Altair of Clouds) bred the dam of Ch. Tumlow Black Magic. This dog in turn sired Ch. Magic Moon of Seale and Ch. Tumlow Magicoat of Seale, breeding back on both sides of the pedigree to Mrs Harris's original mating of Retann Barley Sugar. In 1963 Tumlow Coconut Kisses, daughter of Ch. Tumlow Black Magic, visited Ch. Gisbourne Inca; from this mating the big-winning Ch. Tumlow Fruit Cake was bred. Amongst his many winning progeny can be counted Ch. Imber the Baker's Man, who was bred from a daughter of Ch. Tumlow Magicoat of Seale. The Seale breeding is strongly represented on the tail female side of this dog's pedigree.

Ch. Ritterburg Dark Destiny by William of Ellesmere ex Innishmaan Ebony Eyes of Ritterburg. Owned and bred by Mrs V. Skinner.

Another name to be remembered in the variety is that of Dr Rigg, with the Simonswood prefix. In 1954 he mated a daughter of Ch.s Wylde Cantata and Dusty Shoes of Seale, to the Smooth Ch. Always Popcorn of Thistlehaven (Ch. Silvae Sailor's Quest) and from her bred Ch. Simonswood Sabina. The mating of this bitch to Ch. Altair of Clouds gave him Ch. Simonswood Solange. In all he bred five Wire Champions.

Group Captain and Mrs Satchell cannot be omitted from the records of the winning Wires, for though better known in the Miniature

Ch. Jarthley Nabob
by Ch. Daxene
Yukonly ex Ch.
Mydax Laurer.
Owned and bred by
Mrs J. Lawley.

variety, they owned two home-bred Champions, one of which was Ch.
Orkneyinga Raven, born in 1955 by the sire of Ch. Mordax Miss Mint,
Grunwald Grampion, and ex Orkneyinga Songthrush. Here we find
the Irish kennel of Mrs Huet appearing, for Songthrush was ex I.K.C.
Ch. Greygates Nocturne of Sylvan, by I.K.C. Ch. Brown Boots of
Seale. Mrs Huet founded her line on the Seton-Seale pedigrees and
produced several champions, with Wire blood predominating for many
generations.

Today, the Wire-haired Dachshund has many admirers, his great
appeal being his tremendous sense of fun, sporting character and
willingness to be out and about no matter what the weather. The
club for this variety offers its trophies principally at the Great Joint
Dachshund Championship Show, held in London in the autumn annually. The Kennel Club award twenty two sets of Challenge Certificates
at the various Championship Shows held in England, Wales and Scotland each year, and since 1979 this variety has had certificates on offer
at its own Championship Show.

4 The Miniature Dachshund

At the end of the nineteenth century hunt officials who hunted rabbits on the game reserves in Eastern Germany, owing to the rabbits increasing so rapidly and doing so much damage, decided to breed a very small Teckel that could replace the ferret. Firstly, the popular large Dachshund of the period was mated to miniatures of other breeds, such as Pinschers and Terriers, concentrating on reduction of size and weight. This resulted in a loss of Dachshund type.

By 1905, there could, in a few kennels, be found the results of much work; *pure* bred strains of Zwerg (dwarf) Teckels. In this year the Kaninchen (Rabbit) Teckel Klub was formed. The distinction between these two (according to Dr Schneider Leyer) is that the Zwerg must be able to pursue a fox through tunnels so narrow as to be impassable for a Dachshund of middle weight. The Kaninchen was similarly used for rabbits. In Germany today the weight limit (4 kg) of the little ones has been removed and replaced by the measuring tape. This is taken immediately behind the front legs around the deepest part of the chest, the measure is pulled *very tightly* and the limit for the miniature is 35 centimetres ($13\frac{1}{2}$ in). Living in France at the present time are the Rigol Miniature Wires of Madame Suzanne de Bernes. These included her English Champions Willy Dhu and Phantom Phoebe, who were shown in six different countries and won the highest honours.

The first Miniature Smooths to be recognised in England were those of Lady May Blakiston and Miss A. M. New, in 1925. In that year the Danish Hans von Fehmarn was imported. The following year Bitterlin (also from Denmark) was imported by Lady May and was shown at Cruft's (with no classes for the little ones). The bitch was mated to Hans, and a daughter was retained.

In 1929 Miss Dixon of the Kars prefix imported from Germany an in-whelp bitch, and from this litter Klein Kurio, a small red dog, a typical Dachshund in miniature, was kept. The previous mating of Hans and Bitterlin had resulted in two bitch pups; the one was retained by Lady May and Miss New, the other joining the kennel of Mrs Howard (Seale) who mated her to Klein Kurio.

The Miniature Dachshund Club was formed in 1935, and shortly after this date Miss Dixon, together with Major Reynell, imported a team of Miniature Long Hairs; the Germans had bred from the Zwergs and the Kaninchen Teckels, crossing them with Papillons. These small

Dachshunds proved to be fearless, game and hardy, and as able to stand up to a day's fieldwork as their larger relatives. However, they showed several faults. The coats, though of good length, were too curly and inclined to fluff, heads were short, rather round in skull and snipey in muzzle, eyes were round and full, ears were small and the bodies lacked length, showing clearly that the blood of the Papillon was not far back. The best of the imports was a dog, Halodri von Fleezensee, who was used a great deal at stud. His name can be found in the pedigrees of many of today's kennels if traced far enough back.

The best of the early Miniature Long Hair dogs was probably the son of Halodri, Mrs Herdman's Knowlton Chocolate Soldier. (In the Standard Long Hairs she was doing well with Knowlton Jochen and Madel, the progeny of her import Zola von Jungfrauental). Amongst his progeny was Blümlein of Primrosepatch (ex Zwerg Golden Primrose) this bitch being the foundation of the Robsvarl Miniatures for Mrs Ireland-Blackburne in the year 1936. It was noticeable that the majority of the Miniature breeders were also interested in the Standard variety and had on occasions found very small puppies, both Smooth and Long, in their Standard bred litters. The bitches were not, however, bred from, their owners being under the impression that whelping would be impossible or difficult. The first breeder to mate a very small Standard-bred bitch to the best of the then Miniature dogs was Mrs Smith-Rewse, and she accomplished this with no trouble at whelping, hence Mrs Ireland-Blackburne's Blümlein. These small Standard Miniature crosses, having proved successful, were then mated to pure Miniatures and the stock so bred was of excellent type. The progress made by the Miniature Long Hairs could be traced repeatedly to the Primrosepatch kennel, where their owner mated the best of her small Standard blood lines to the best of the Miniatures.

The Smooth Miniature breeders were reluctant to use the Standard blood lines to improve their stock, though they did on occasion use a Long Hair Miniature to improve both the bone and the ribbing.

In 1948 the Kennel Club granted a separate register for both the Smooth and the Long Hair, with Challenge Certificates granted in the following year. Up till then the Miniatures could only win Challenge Certificates in competition with the Standards, this had been done by Mrs Smith-Rewse with Primrosepatch Miss Mouse (Standard-bred), Mrs Portman Graham with Ch. Marcus of Mornyvarna (registered as Standard and then transferred to the Miniature register), and Mrs Bailey's Ch. Adrelson Gold Orchid. With the opening of separate breed status, the Miniature Long Hair went ahead in leaps and bounds. Mrs Bellamy of the von Walders owned the first bitch Champion in Ch. Chloe von Walder in 1948, with Ch. Marcus of Mornyvarna as the first of the dog Champions. Robsvarl Redwing bred Ch. Robsvarl Red

Robin, who appears in countless pedigrees of the present day winning stock, both Smooth and Long. Mrs Smith-Rewse had many great Champions, and supplied the foundation stock for many breeders at home and abroad. The Mornyvarnas bred several Certificate winners but are best known for the stud achievements of Ch. Marcus, who sired no less than eight full Champions. From him Mr and Mrs Buck of the Buckmead Standards bred their lovely Ch. Miss Miniver, not Miniature but small Standard, who won her Championship against her larger sisters.

Mrs Bellamy continued to breed top-flight Miniatures and had several Champions to her credit, amongst them being Ch. and American Ch. Mighty Fine von Walder. Mrs Connell's (of the von Holzners) foundation Amanda of Primrosepatch is behind Ch. Martin von Holzner and his daughter Ch. Modern Millie.

A bitch of importance for the pedigrees of the early 1950s is to be found in Ch. Priorsgate Miss Muffet; she appears as dam of both Ch. Priorsgate Tom Thumb and Ch. Priorsgate Yvonne. The breeding of Miss Muffet is mainly that of Primrosepatch, so combining the Standard and the Miniature Long blood.

The Hoylins of Miss Mary Fletcher in the mid-50s were bred from the Mornyvarna and the Primrosepatch blood-lines. The better known of these, Ch. and Irish Ch. Jeremy Fisher of Hoylin, appears as great grandsire of Mrs Oswell's stud dog Ch. Mertynabbott Byworth Comet, who was the sire or grandsire of practically all the Mertynabbott Champions.

Mrs Gwyer of the Marlenwoods consistently bred from her Champions Jamie and Jon a long line of good bitches, who can be seen in the extended pedigrees of today's show exhibits. Ch. Priorsgate Marlenwood Royce is behind the well known (in the late 60s) Armorel dogs and bitches of Mr and Mrs Stevenson through his son, Ch. Springmount Madrigal; again, all these extended pedigrees show the Primrosepatch influence.

Behind the winning Brigmerstons were the Marlenwoods, the von Walders and the Robsvarls. This is through an earlier mating of a lightweight, to the Miniature Ch. Moselle von Walder, to produce Reedscottage (Lady Kathleen Hare) Rattan, who appears as sire to the well known Ch. Delphik Derry in the ownership of Mr and Mrs Fielding.

Ch. Delphik Derry, through his son Ch. Delphik Donamos, was grandsire to the lovely multiple Certificate-winner Ch. Delphik Debrett. This beautiful bitch had for two years, 1969 and 1970, been awarded the Dachshund Club's Ch. Jackdaw Trophy, which is won by the dog or bitch of any variety of Dachshund winning the most points during the year. Ch. Derry sired eleven Champion progeny.

Ch. Delphik
Debrett by Ch.
Delphik Donamos
ex Ch. Delphik
Dhobi. Owned and
bred by Mr and Mrs
Fielding.

Debrett was mated to Ch. Delphik Diplomatic by Ch. Delphik
Derry, and whelped Ch Delphik Distinguished. Mrs Fielding pur-
chased from the owner of the silver dapple Ch. Littlenodes Silver
Smoke (Mrs Owen), a silver dapple bitch, and made her up as the first
Dapple Champion bitch Antrobus Silver Sparkle of Delphik. She was
bred by Mrs Gregory ex Hilgreg Holly Queen, this bitch carrying Ch.
Mertynabbot Byworth Comet and Primrosepatch blood.

Ch. Wildstar
Wizzard by Ch.
Rhinestar Southern
Comfort ex Wildstar
Sweet Sensation.
Owned and bred by
Mr R. Wood.

A very strong kennel which began to make its presence felt in the early 60s was that of Mrs Parsons, with the prefix Minutist. Her background was that of Robsvarl and Marlenwood. Many Champions at home and in America carry his prefix.

The Minutists, no longer being bred by Mrs Parsons can, however, be found in the pedigrees of the Ridgeviews of Mrs Wilson. Her first Champion, Ridgeview Romeo by Minutist Costa ex Ridgeview Rachel, (Minutist both sides) was followed by Ch. Tupee Tweedledee of Ridgeview, this one by English and S. African Ch. Minutist Ottoman, ex Littlenodes Black Tulip (by the silver dapple Littlenodes Quick Silver). History was made by Mrs Wilson in that she bred and showed to his Championship Ridgeview Dark Brown Tweed, the first chocolate and tan Long coat to achieve a title. This dog continued the Minutist line on both sides of the pedigree.

Further descendants of the Minutists could be found in the Bushcots; Ch. Bushcot Hazel had, in the first three generations, only two names not Minutist. Hazel leads on to the Rhinestars, the first of them to become a Champion was Rhinestar Dedication by Ch. Sunara Sorrento ex a Woodreed bitch. This same dam when mated to Ch. Buscot Dandelion of Rhinestar whelped Ch. Rhinestar Buttercup. The Beltrims of Mrs Cole-Hamilton, through Ch. Minutist Casino, bred Ch. Beltrim Carlo.

The present-day owner of the Primrosepatch prefix is the niece of Mrs Smith-Rewse, Mrs Sidgwick, who made up in the mid-50s. Ch. Primrosepatch Lady Brown, by Primrosepatch Tiny Man, a son of Ch. Robsvarl Red Robin ex Primrosepatch Fairy Fay, her dam by Red Robin ex the first Miniature of the variety to win a Challenge Certificate, Primrosepatch Miss Mouse (by Primrosepatch Red Lancer). Lady Brown, when mated to Ch. Jeremy Fisher of Hoylin, bred the dam of Ch. Wenbarn Peregrine, sire of Mrs Blandford's big winner, Ch. Mertynabbot Lancelot. Ch. Brigmerston Lord Chares of Primrosepatch is carrying Ch. Delphik Derry as grandparent with Ch. Ravenhead Anna as grandam (Robsvarl, Marlenwood and von Walder). The original prefix is far back in his pedigree.

Descending from Ch. Mertynabbot Lancelot we find the Jackanordies of Mrs Wakefield. The first of her Champions, Jackanordie Jolyon, was followed by Ch. Jackanordie Digby and Ch. Jackanordie Val 'N' Tine. From Ch. Jolyon Mr Crawford bred Ch. Voryn's Joseph ex a Primrosepatch bitch.

The Standard Long Hair Ch. Imber Coffee Bean can also be found in the extended pedigrees of the Sunara kennel. His great-great-granddaughter Imber Demi Tasse represents a combination of Primrosepatch, Mornyvarna and the Marlenwood through her dam – a daughter of Ch. Espeejay Sunglow (when mated to a lightweight Coffee

Ch. Sunara Sea Symphony by Ch. Sunara Sorrento ex Ch. Sunara Royal Artist. Owned and bred by Mrs Fraser Gibson.

Bean daughter). Demi Tasse, when mated to Sunara Mertynabbot Goblin, bred Ch. Sunara Sorrento, who later became top stud with innumerable Champion offspring. Demi Tasse, when mated to Minutist Diabolo, had a daughter who achieved her title as Sunara Gloire of Dijon. The sire of Demi Tasse was Bordak Forestford Fine Fettle. Mr and Mrs Fraser Gibson exported to California a half brother of Sorrento, Sunara Firecracker, a dog much used at stud in the U.S.A. The type produced by him is dissimilar to the Sorrento stock – probably the result of the 10 lb weight limit. Those whom I have seen pictured in the glossy illustrations in the *American Dachshund* are taller on the leg and have not got the bone or depth of body of those seen here.

The Sunaras are behind many big winners in a number of kennels, in particular the Southcliffs of Alan Sharman, so carrying on the influence of the Smooth Standard imported from Austria in 1938, Ch. Zeus vom Schwarenberg. This dog not only influenced the Standard Smooths and Longs (refer to Anneliese Wurm's article), but through the recessive Long Haired dog Imber Black Coffee (the recessive great-great-great-grandson) to his son Coffee Bean, and so via Demi Tasse to the Miniature Longs.

Mrs Beryl Castle had been interested in Miniatures for a long while, and had been very successful with her Smooths and Wires. She had great difficulty in breeding top-flight Miniature Longs, but she did this in no small measure with the arrival of Ch. Cannobio Sukina. She amassed many certificates including B.I.S. at Breed Championship shows. She ended 1978 with the award of a new trophy from the Dachshund Club, the Amyas Biss and Bob Gale Trophy, and was runner-up to the Club's Jackdaw Trophy, which is for the top winner in all coats. The breeding of Sukina is interesting in that it represents the crossing of the Smooth and Long coats; this was before the Kennel Club restrictions. Sukina's grandparents on the dam's side being the Smooth Dalegarth Dominick (Ch. Dalegarth Dabster ex Dalegarth Lizette) and Bardival Little May (Miniature Long by Delrene Golden Sovereign ex Bramble of Bardival.) The daughter of Dominick and Little May, a Smooth, registered as Cannobio Sweet Dessert, was mated to the Miniature Long, Ridgeview Ruggles, himself Long-Hair-bred, and with Minutist grandparents on the dam's side.

Ch. Cannobio Sukina by Ridgeview Ruggles ex Cannobio Sweet Dessert. Owned and bred by Mrs Beryl

The Miniature long-haired Dachshund has a great number of enthusiasts at the present time. In the show ring the classes are well filled, and the registrations are large and increasing yearly.

The Miniature Smooth traces back to the importation in 1929 of Klein Kurio, and also to the importation from Denmark four years earlier of Hans von Fehmarn and as mate for him – Bitterlin. Lady May Blakiston and Miss New, the owners of this pair, kept from one of the early litters a bitch who was mated more than once to her sire. In 1936 a daughter of Hans and Bitterlin was taken by them to the Long Hair, Piccolo of Brenvil. To quote from Miss New, 'We did this mating with the sole object of improving the type of the Smooth Miniatures at that time, which were mostly high on the leg, poor-boned and apple-headed. We had seen Miniature Long Hairs at shows and noticed they had better bone and feet, were lower to ground and with better heads.'

Mrs Howard of the Seale suffix had also had one of the bitches from Hans and Bitterlin whom she mated to Klein Kurio, retaining Minnie Mouse of Seale. The little bitch was later mated to Mrs Howard's import, Maiklang aus dem Lohegau, and bred Caesar of Seale. An earlier mating in 1933 of the bitch Madi von der Jeetzel of Seale gave Mrs Howard Gentian of Seale who, when mated to Maiklang aus dem Lohegau, produced Marmaduke of Seale. The latter was mated to Taschen Panda and sired Taschen Tango who appears as both sire of Minivale Larita and grandsire of Minivale Masterpiece – the foundations of the Minivale line for Mrs Winder. The Taschen prefix of Lady May Blakiston and Miss New was not registered until 1936; consequently the foundation bitch bred by them and owned by Mrs Howard did not bear their prefix. From a mating done by them in 1936 of the Smooth and Long, all the puppies had, of course, been Smooth but carrying the Long Hair factor. In a subsequent mating of one of the dogs back to his grandam, a Long Hair dog was amongst the litter of four, he being registered as Taschen Trustful. In the pedigree of Ch. Taschen Tappet, her dam Taschen Tippet has one grandparent, the Long Hair Trustful, mated to the Ch. and Irish Ch. Jeremy Fisher of Hoylin, resulting in the Long Hair Ch. Tappet.

The Montreux kennel of Mr Negal is in part descended from Maiklang aus dem Lohegau, through a son of this dog ex Zwerg of Teeflette (imported by Major Reynell around 1930). From this mating he kept Mauretania of Montreux, who later mated a very small black and tan bitch with the Montreux suffix, a dog, Black Watch of Montreux, being retained. In 1945 Mr Negal picked, from a litter of Standard Smooths, a small chocolate and tan bitch (the sire a lightweight import, and the dam a daughter of the famous Ch. Zeus vom Schwarenberg). She was later mated to his pre-war dog, the aforementioned Black Watch. This mating became the foundation to his successful strain through their daughter Titania and their son Prince John.

Contessina of Montreux became the first Miniature bitch Champion in 1948, and was mated to her son Prince John to make a dominant type for this kennel. From this mating Ch. Stephan of Montreux was bred, having outstanding bone and substance with a wonderful head, and was quite a different type to the Miniature Smooths of that day. Mr Negal mated him to a daughter of Prince John (double line-breeding) and produced a tiny bitch who at maturity weighed 9 lb. She became Ch. Mariella of Montreux. For her mating she visited Ch. Merryweather Marvel – a son of Mrs Winder's Ch. Minivale Melvin who was the progeny of a brother and sister mating, these two being the grandchildren of the first of the Minivales, Masterpiece, he in turn being grandson of the import Maiklang aus dem Lohegau. Ch. Mariella and Ch. Merryweather Marvel's son, Cassandra of Montreux, was the sire of Titania's litter in which the black and tan dog Romulus of Montreux was bred. He appears in the pedigrees of many of the Montreux Champions and of Champions to be found in other kennels.

Mrs Winder, with Ch. Minivale Melvin and his sire Ch. Minivale Miraculous, did a great deal of big winning around the early 1950s, and indeed provided the foundation bitch for Mrs Littmoden's Wendlitt kennel. This is through Minivale Majestic, the sire of Miraculous, grandsire of Melvin and sire of Ch. Minivale Matinee Girl, Mrs Littmoden mated her in 1953 back to the double grandson of Majestic, Ch. Minivale Melvin, and bred the lovely Ch. Otter of Wendlitt. Ch. Melvin appears in strength behind Mrs Bassett's Ch.s Marvel and Magic, the litter brothers, whose dam Ch. Merryweather Matilda was a daughter of the sire of Melvin, Ch. Miraculous. Many of the Champions in this period contain the Minivales in their pedigrees. Ch. Merryweather Matilda was the foundation bitch of Mrs Bassett's kennel. She became the grandam of ten Champions.

Ch. Minivale Matinee Girl, apart from whelping Ch. Otter, bred Ch.s Gaiety Girl and Career Girl for Mrs Littmoden, when mated to Ch. Melvin. Ch. Gaiety Girl, when mated to the Ch. Stephan of Montreux's son, Puck of Wendlitt, sired Jack-a-dandy of Wendlitt, the sire of Ch. Dandy Dan. This stud dog made a great name for himself by siring the multiple Certificate winner Ch. Prince Albert of Wendlitt, the dam introducing yet another well-known kennel in Ch. Wendlitt Tessa of Hobbithill. Tessa was a daughter of Ch. Hannah of Hobbithill sired by Ch. Merryweather Magic. The last-named dog was an exceptionally good sire, his name appearing in the pedigrees of the Limberins of Mr Hague was sire of Ch.s Pimpernel and Penny Black (litter mates), and also as the paternal grandsire of these two, and behind the outstanding sire of Champions, Ch. Limberin Americano; this latter dog had Ch. Minivale Miraculous as paternal grandsire.

Mr Hague had bred down from his Standard stock to produce his consistent strain of big winners. The dog he rated very highly is Ch. Americano (sire of six Champions). The Standard blood is represented in his early 1960 pedigrees by the mating of Limberin Lucy Locket to the small Ch. Deetails Request, a son of the exceptional sire Ch. Silvae Sailor's Quest. From this union he retained the 13 lb Limberin Lilting Lullaby, mating her to a son of Ch. Merryweather Magic to breed Limberin Firefly, then mating her to her grandsire Magic to produce Penny Black and Pimpernel.

An earlier mating had been to the Ch. Magic brother, Ch. Marvel, producing Ch. Limberin Marienina, Americano being a son of Firefly and Ch. Minivale President who in turn was a son of Ch. Miraculous ex the granddaughter of Ch. Merryweather Magic. He is the sire of, amongst other Champions, Ch. Winston of Hobbithill (grandson Ch.

Magic), Winston being sire of the lovely Ch. Limberin Honour Bright, the distinguished winner of a Championship Show Hound Group, and also of his double granddaughter, Ch. Limberin Tarantella.

The Limberins continued to occupy the top spot in the ring with Ch. Golden Glory, a double granddaughter of Americano: Ch. Pan American, and, in the last years of his life, Limberin Xtremely won the Puppy Stakes at the Welsh Kennel Club.

From the Limberins and the Hobbithills we get the Roslayes and the Braishvales; Ch. Prince Albert when mated to Roslaye Bubbles produced Ch. Roslaye Rigby, himself siring Ch. Roslaye Ruggles and Ch. Roslaye Calypso Girl. The Braishvales came through Hobbithill Arabella, dam of Ch. Dormy Frederick of Wendlitt and Braishvale Lively Lady, daughter of Ch. Prince Albert, and granddaughter of Ch. Wendlitt Tessa of Hobbithill. This mating gave two Champions, Braishvale Jumping Jack and Braishvale Star of Redcliffe. Amongst Jumping Jack's outstanding progeny are Dr Kershaw's Ch. Hobbithill Zephania, and Mrs Pugh's Ch. Hobbithill Zebedee of Tarkotta.

Behind the Amberleighs of Mesdames Angus and Evans we find Ch. Limberin Topper. Also at the back of the pedigree of Lady Dick Lauder's Willowfields is Ch. Topper. Ch. Willowfield Woodcock (now in New Zealand) has for his dam a granddaughter of that dog, Amberleigh Amaryllis. Ch. About Turn of Amberleigh is grandson of Ch. Merryweather Masquerade, son of Ch. Merryweather Moreover. Amaryllis, when mated to Ch. Wimoway William Tell, whelped Mrs Bassett's Ch. Willowfield Sweet William – a bitch.

During 1954 Ch. Otter of Wendlitt (Ch. Minivale Melvin and Ch. Minivale Matinee Girl's son) sired a bitch soon to become the foundation of the kennel of Mr and Mrs Newbury under the prefix Dalegarth. Ch. Dalegarth Teilwood Sally bred, when mated to Jack-a-Dandy of Wendlitt, Ch. Dalegarth Dabster, and later, mated to her son, bred Ch. Dalegarth Designer. Ch. Dabster sired Ch. Dalegarth Charlie Brown, who, when mated to a Ch. Dabster daughter, bred Dalegarth Charleston. In 1967 a Ch. Dabster daughter mated to a Ch. Charlie Brown son, bred Ch. Dalegarth Lichen.

At this time the Dalegarths were living in Ireland and Ch. Dabster, at the age of 13, was fortuitously mated to a Miniature Wire bitch. Ch. Dabster can be found behind the winning exhibits from the Cannobio kennel of Mrs Castle. Ch. Cannobio Silken Tassle is by Ch. Dalegarth Designer, and Ch. Cannobio So Smart and Ch. Cannobio School Marm both by another Ch. Dabster son, Dalegarth Dominick.

Mr and Mrs Smith were yet another kennel to have bred down from the Standards, this through Silvae Outline. Ch. Washington Rose, when mated to the big winning Ch. Bowbank Red Riordan, whelped Ch. Wimoway Water Lily.

Ch. Hobbithill
Zephania by Ch.
Braishvale Jumping
Jack ex Hobbithill
Polly.
Owned and bred
by Dr Kershaw.

Ch. Pipersvale
Pina-Colada by Ch.
Monksmile
Dan-De-Lion ex
Ch. Pipersvale
Beaujolais. Owned
and bred by Mrs B.
Munt. Winner of
more Challenge
Certificates than any
other dog of any
breed.

Mr and Mrs Smith's Wimoway kennel bred their first Champion,
Ch. Wimoway Washington Rose, ex a Dabster daughter by Mrs Bland-
ford's Ch. Flaunden Senator (a Ch. Romulus of Montreux son). The
Wimoways continue their winning ways, descending from Ch. Water-

lily through her grandson Ch. Wimoway William Tell. Through his grandfather we find a Montreux, Hobart, a black and tan, behind many Champions, in particular Mr and Mrs Smith's Ch. Luxonfield Black Magic of Wimoway. This lovely girl is a daughter of Luxonfield Nutty ex Roslaye Bettina (with Hobart as grandsire). Hobart is also sire of Ch. Wimoway Chocolate Soldier. Ch. Black Magic became the dam of five champions.

Ch. Dalegarth Girl Friday by Ch. Berrycourt Blackthorn ex Dalegarth Sallyforth. Owned and bred by Mr and Mrs F. Newbury.

The Cannobios of Mrs Castle made a significant contribution to the advance of this variety; probably the best-known being Ch. Cannobio School Marm.

Mrs Basset's Ch. Merryweather Marvel sired, amongst others, Ch. Merryweather Matthew, who in turn when mated to a Ch. Magic daughter Limpsfield Topaz, bred Ch. Merryweather Murgatroyd and Ch. Merryweather Marcello. Ch. Merryweather Matthew is in the pedigrees of the Potsdowns of Mr and Mrs Woollam, firstly as double grandsire of Ch. Potsdown Morgan, who is the sire of Ch. Potsdown Limelight. Ch. Murgatroyd can be seen as grandsire of Ch. Vienda Kitty Fisher. He also appears behind Ch. Bowbank Red Riordan as great-grandsire when mated to the Ch. Romulus of Montreux, daughter of Ch. Chocoletta of Montreux.

Over the years since the early 1950s the Limpsfield kennel of Miss Molesworth had consistently bred really small stock, and bitches bred by her are to be found in the extended pedigrees of many of today's winners. In particular, Mrs Bassett's Ch. Merryweather Matilda was ex Limpsfield Miss Meickle, a daughter of Ch. Minivale Melvin, Mrs

Samuel's Ch. Trudie of Bettmark ex Limpsfield Garnet, while Ch. Merryweather Murgatroyd was the son of Limpsfield Topaz. Mrs Samuel's Ch. Trudie bred Ch. Truelove of Bettmark, sired by yet another Limpsfield, Early Bird. Ch. Truelove whelped Ch. Merryweather Mills, this dog making history by siring Ch. Merryweather Moreover when mated to a Ch. Merryweather Magic daughter.

In 1965, through the mating of a daughter of Ch. Otter of Wendlitt to Ch. Moreover, Mrs Gracy's Ch. Runnel Petticoat came into the picture. She became the winner in 1967 of the Dachshund Club's Jackdaw Trophy and the winner of eighteen Challenge Certificates.

Ch. Berrycourt Blackthorn by Ch. Braishvale Crackerjack ex Berrycourt Morning Star. Owned and bred by Mr and Mrs R. Voaden.

A kennel which bred down from the Standards is that of the Booths of Mrs Foden. She had previously been successful with the larger relations. Her first Miniature to achieve high honours was through the mating of a Ch. Minivale Miraculous grandson, Sheumac Skeeter, to a lightweight daughter of Ch. Hawkstone Superb, this resulting in the crowning of Ch. Booth Minnehaha in 1964. In the same year Mrs Foden made up another Ch. Miraculous granddaughter, this one being sired by Zebo of Bettmark (a Ch. Magic grandson). In the following year she also made up Ch. Booth Christina, a Ch. Merryweather Moreover daughter.

The Pipersvales and the Bowbanks of Mrs Munt and Mrs Solomon combine their owners' pedigree dogs. Ch. Tia Maria of Pipersvale being by Ch. Bowbank Drambuie ex Pipersvale Penelope Ann, whose sire is Drambuie, a son of Ch. Bowbank Red Riley and dam Penelope

Jane, a daughter of Prince Charles of Wendlitt (Ch. Dandy Dan and Ch. Wendlitt Tessa of Hobbithill). Mrs Munt's Ch. Bowbank Drambuie is sire of Ch. Bowbank Tamarisk and Teazel and of Ch. Royal Brandy of Pipersvale, who is in turn sire to Ch. Pipersvale Summer Breeze ex Bowbank Summer Sunshine.

Mr and Mrs Fox of the Shepherdsdene affix had as their foundation a dog, Trinket of Bletchingham, three generations removed from Klein Kurio. They mated him to a Miniature bitch of Seale breeding and retained Shepherdsdene Brilliant: this was the start of their red line. Later Trinket was mated to the German-bred Melitta of Tootysfield, and the whole litter was bought in. The bitch of this mating, Gem of Shepherdsdene, was bred to Brilliant, thus line-breeding to Trinket of Bletchingham. The kennel has now reached its twelfth generation of red stock; the dog Ch. Shepherdsdene Pippin represents the fourth generation in a line of Champion dogs, carrying, in the extended pedigree, Miraculous and also Ch. Merryweather Magic. Apart from these two studs the Shepherdsdene pedigrees consist of home-bred stock and this bred continuously. They have eight Champions to their credit, seven of them dogs.

The kennel houses the unusual colour of fawn (with black points) amongst its inmates. These have been bred from the reds, and must represent a weakening of the pigment, though retaining the dark eyes and nails which are so essential.

I have only mentioned a very few of the Miniature Smooth breeders. There are, of course, many more. The background is mainly the German imports, combined with the Minivales who were founded on the Danish imports of the early 1920s, not forgetting the lightweight Smooths who so frequently appear far back in the pedigrees.

Shortly after the 1939–45 war, Sir Charles Lambe and Mr and Mrs Adrian Molony (Huntersbroad) became interested in trying to establish Miniature Wire-haired Dachshunds.

Sir Charles Lambe (Dunkerque) had a bitch, Kiwi, who consistently whelped in each litter remarkably small puppies. Kiwi weighed 14 lb, though bred from Standard stock. In 1950 she was mated to a Miniature Smooth dog, and from this mating a Wire Hair, Nutmeg of Dunkerque, $11\frac{1}{2}$ lb, was retained. Mrs Molony became the owner and Nutmeg thus became one of the foundation bitches of this line. Later, when mated to Silver Prince of Seale, a lightweight Smooth, Huntersbroad Fox Hunter, a Miniature Smooth dapple, and Huntersbroad Duffle, a Miniature Red Wire were kept.

In 1950 Mr Molony imported from Germany the dogs Barro aus der Waidmannsklause and Max von Wallpromenade, and also the bitch Aggi (Schmitz) who was the second foundation bitch of the Huntersbroad kennel, Aggi weighing $10\frac{3}{4}$ lb and dapple in colour.

The mating of Barro and Aggi produced Huntersbroad Graphite, a 14 lb silver dapple Wire Hair, a dog who proved to be one of the most important stud dogs. Mrs Besson of the Ballyteckel kennels in Ireland owned Jeda of Ballyteckel, a small Standard Wire by the famous Ch. Midas of Seton, son of the Irish Ch. Paganini of Seton, a grandson of the lovely Swedish importation Sports Silence of Seton. Jeda was mated to Barro; from the mating Ballyteckel Thornbarton Faddle was retained and later mated to Huntersbroad Graphite, thus bringing Barro into the pedigree as double grandsire; a daughter was kept by Mrs Besson and mated to her sire, Graphite. A dog from this litter joined the kennel in Finland of Mr Hackman, Chairman of the Finnish Dachshund Club. A bitch, Huntersbroad Harriet, became the foundation of the Orkneyinga Miniature Wires, property of Group Captain and Mrs Satchell.

Max von Wallpromenade was unfortunately killed shortly after leaving quarantine, and his only mating, to a lightweight Smooth, Gretel of Cisne (a red), produced the foundation bitch, in Wega of Cisne, for Mme Suzanne de Bernes. Wega was mated to Graphite, and two puppies, the black and tan Wire Rigol Susie's Liquorice, and the red Wire dapple Rigol Susie's Fudge, were the start, both in England and on the Continent, of the most successful Rigol line. Rigol Susie's Fudge, in the ownership of Mr Colbourne, was mated to Huntersbroad Firefly (Graphite and Plover by Barro ex Aggi) and in the issue was Redenhall Silver Wings and Redenhall Gold Braid.

Mme de Bernes twice mated Rigol Susie's Liquorice to Redenhall Silver Wings. From the first litter came Rigol Phantom Philip and from the second Ch. Rigol Willy Dhu.

Redenhall Gold Braid was bred by Mr Colbourne from the mating of Rigol Susie's Fudge to Huntersbroad Firefly and subsequently mated to Paulette of Sillwood, the foundation bitch of Squadron Leader and Mrs Whitehouse, she being a daughter of Sillwood Paula of Dunkerque, by the Miniature Smooth Minivale William ex the 14 lb Kiwi of Dunkerque. Sqn Ldr and Mrs Whitehouse bred three Champions from this mating, the first litter producing Ch. Gold Bracken of Granta, the second Ch. Teak of Granta and Ch. Gold Ilex of Granta.

Mrs Jean Blandford, with the Flaunden prefix, acquired, in 1961, from his breeders Sqn Ldr and Mrs Whitehouse, a dog soon to become Ch. Teak of Granta. His sire was the prepotent stud Redenhall Gold Braid, with the dam the foundation bitch of his breeders, Paulette of Seale (Kiwi of Dunkerque as maternal grandam). The little dog was full brother to Ch. Gold Ilex of Granta. He sired in 1962 Ch. Flaunden Wentworth ex a Merryweather Moustachio daughter. Ch. Wentworth later appeared as grandsire to Ch. Flaunden the Whitehouse. Mrs Blandford mated the dam of Ch. Flaunden the Whitehouse for a subsequent litter to Ch. Redenhall Yewberry and bred the outstanding Ch. Flaunden Wimpole Street.

Mrs Collins and Miss Cook owned in partnership the Champion son of Rigol Phantom Philip ex a daughter of Mr Colbourne's Redenhall Gold Braid, the silver dapple Ch. Kelvindeugh Lauder Likely. Mrs Flynn of the Culdees Standard and Miniature Wires bred Ch. and Australian Ch. Culdees Ulric from Rigol Rough Shod, a great grandson of Redenhall Gold Braid, and grandson of Phantom Philip.

Miss Gray of the Paxfords bred her first Champion Miniature Wire through using a dog bred by Mr Colbourne, Ch. Redenhall Yewberry. The pedigree of this dog shows Redenhall Gold Braid and Paulette of Sillwood as great-grandparents on the dam's side, with the Smooth Ch. Flaunden Senator as grandparent on the sire's side. Ch. Yewberry proved himself an excellent sire in the ownership of Mrs Lawley.

Mrs Ruth Spong with the Peredur prefix is continually breeding good small stock of excellent type. Her foundation bitch was the lightweight Standard Wire, Simonswood Sylphine, the daughter of two Champions. The bitch, when mated to Group Captain and Mrs Satchell's Orkneyinga Oscar, a son of the import Orkneyinga Jockele vom Furstenfels (himself a son of Barro aus der Waidmannsklause), and ex Huntersbroad Harriet, whelped the bitches Orkneyinga Nereid and Ch. Orkneyinga Nerina. The latter, mated to Ch. Orkneyinga Red Gauntlet, a son of Orkneyinga Oscar, bred Orkneyinga Vottr. For Mrs Spong, Orkneyinga Nereid bred Ch. Peredur Pimento, the sire of, amongst other good winners, Mrs Hood-Wright's lovely Ch. Selwood Marguerite, and Ch. Peredur Sinful Skinful. This particular pedigree shows the mating of son to mother, i.e. Ch. Pimento to Nereid. Ch. Marguerite brings another kennel name into the picture, that of Bluefelt. This kennel had previously concentrated on the Standard Wires. Mrs Taylor had obtained a small Wire, Lapwing of Fellisfield, a double granddaughter of the 14 lb Kiwi of Dunkerque, and from her bred Ch. Bluefelt Honeysuckle of Darlaston.

Mrs Rhodes bought from Mrs Besson of Ireland, Ballyteckel Walt Weevil, a son of Huntersbroad Minoru, a grandson of Barro aus der Waidmannsklause, and Aggi (Schmitz). Her dam, Ballyteckel Win Wireworm, was sired by Huntersbroad Graphite ex the Barro/Jeda of Ballyteckel daughter. Coobeg Ballyteckel Walt Weevil became the first of the Miniature Wire Champion dogs. He sired for Mrs Rhodes Ch. Coobeg Punch.

Mrs Wakefield of the Sillwood suffix, a breeder of Miniature Smooths, became interested in the Miniature Wires, breeding in 1957 the first Miniature Wire Champion bitch in Ch. Jane of Sillwood. She was bred from three lines of Smooth breeding, with the fourth that from the little Kiwi of Dunkerque whose daughter Paula of Dunkerque, when mated to Liseson of Sillwood, bred Ch. Jane. She later was mated to Moat Rumpelstiltskin (Barro ex the Miniature Smooth Shepherdsdene Gold Bar), so breeding Paulette of Silwood, previously mentioned as the foundation of Sqn Ldr and Mrs Whitehouse's successful kennel.

In the late sixties another kennel was forging ahead, that of the Silvaes of Mrs Grosvenor Workman. Ch. Redenhall Yewberry had mated a Ch. Peredur Pimento daughter, Monteagle Betsy Trotwood, by Orkneyinga Oscar ex a Moat Rumpelstiltskin bitch. From this union came Ch. Silvae the Mouse, the first of a line of outstanding Miniature Wires. When mated to Ch. Bryn of Paxford (Ch. Redenhall Yewberry ex the Ch. Peredur Pimento daughter ex Ch. Peredur Wee Taffy of Paxford) amongst other winning stock in the litter, Ch. Silvae Enormouse was soon crowned.

Silvae Itsamouse, daughter of Ch. Redenhall Yewberry, when mated to Ch. Witch Doctor of Cumtru, whelped Silvae Mandymouse. She became the foundation of Mrs Zena Andrews's Drakesleats. She was mated to Selwood Penstemon, becoming dam of Ch. Drakesleat Hussy. Hussy for her first mating when to Ch. Selwood Dittany bringing into the pedigree of the offspring Ch. Peredur Pimento – twice. From this mating came Drakeslet Klunk Klick who became a Champion with

Drakesleat
Champions:
Ch. Riff Raff,
Ch. Kalamity Kate,
Ch. Scarlet Woman
Ch. Klunk Klick.

Miss Raphael's suffix added to his name. This little dog won many Certificates and awards in the Hound Group. Hussy, when mated to Drakesleat Range Rover, whelped Ch. Drakesleat Miss Alliance and had the Brackenacre suffix attached to her name, and when mated to Ch. Silvae Handymouse bred Ch. Drakesleat Scarlet Woman. Amongst the top wins for this kennel we find their record of best Miniature Wire at Cruft's for four years. The first of these was Ch. Drakesleat Kalamity Kate, the second Ch. Drakesleat Klunk Klick of Andyc, in Miss Raphael's ownership, and then repeating this in 1977. In the following year Ch. Drakesleat Ali Jail went on to win Reserve in the Hound Group.

The Silvaes continue with the Mouse family, and are always well to the fore. The latest contenders are a son of Ch. Silvae Crazymouse and Ch. Silvae Cider – she bringing in Ch. Peredur Wee Taffy of Paxford and Kelvindeugh Lauder Laurel by Ch. Bryn of Paxford – and Ch. Silvae Scrumpy by Ch. Silvae Rubbermouse ex Ch. Silvae Cider.

Ch. Silvae Handymouse by Ch. Selwood Dittany ex Silvae Itsa-mouse is the property of Mrs Brown in Auckland, New Zealand.

Miss Raphael (Andyc), apart from her big wins with Ch. Drakesleat Klunk Klick of Andyc, constantly brings into the ring very typical little animals (she had as a stud force Ch. Selwood Dittany) and with the descendants of Ch. Bryn of Paxford (Ch.s Andyc Topper and Tansy) is a kennel to be reckoned with.

In 1971 Mrs O. McLean, an enthusiastic breeder in Ulster, mated

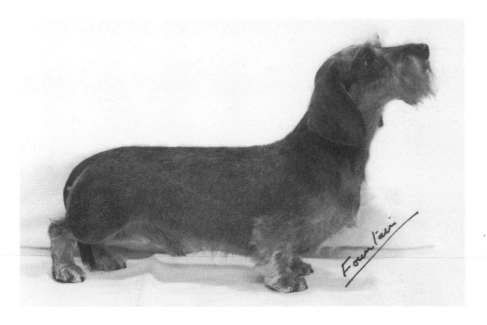

Ch. Selwood Dittany by Peredur Oddjob ex Sellwood Buttercup. Owned by Miss Raphael. Bred by Mrs P. Hood-Wright.

a Miniature Wire bitch, Pink String of Cumtru, to the Smooth Miniature Ch. Dalegarth Dabster, who was then thirteen years old. The whole litter was wire-coated and Mr and Mrs Newbury acquired from the litter a bitch, Beannchor Dormouse, possessing the forechest and hind angulation for which Dabster had previously appeared to be prepotent. Dormouse, when mated to Miss Raphael's Ch. Selwood Dittany, produced Dalegarth Keyman, an outcross foundation for the Dalegarth Miniature Wires. To intensify the Dabster type, Keyman was mated to his litter sister and also to his dam. From these matings came Ch. Dalegarth Jus' William and Ch. Dalegarth Ragamuffin respectively.

Mrs Castle mated Dalegarth Thankful to Mrs E. Blackburn's Ch. Stargang Badger – by Ch. Bryn of Paxford ex a granddaughter of Pink String of Cumtru – breeding Ch. Cannobio Witches Brew, and a Dalegarth Keyman daughter returned to her sire to produce Ch. Cannobio Teddy Bear.

Mrs Willoughby of the suffix Cumtru had been breeding consistently for many years a really good type of Miniature Wire, many of them dapple in colouring. She made up Witch Doctor of Cumtru to Championship status, and several in her kennel were Certificate winners.

The miniature Wires are going from strength to strength. When they were first exhibited in the early 1950s, the weight for the show ring was 12 lb and under. Aggi (Schmitz) at maturity turned the scales at $10\frac{3}{4}$ lb; she unfortunately was soon out of the ring owing to the loss

Ch. Dalegarth Ruff 'N Tumble by Dalegarth Dee Jay ex Dalegarth Thyme. Owned and bred by Mr and Mrs F. Newbury.

of two teeth whilst out hunting. Her fame has been assured through her mating to Barro aus der Waidmannsklause, to produce Huntersbroad Graphite, the silver dapple sire and grandsire *par excellence*. His is the same name behind the success of the Rigols, the Ballyteckels, the Orkneyingas (through Huntersbroad Harriet), the two Seale Champions Omah and O'Kay, also the Grantas and, through them, the big winning kennel of Mrs Jean Blandford's Flaundens. The Gisbournes of Mrs Quick can be traced to Graphite through the Ballyteckels and the Paxfords through the Peredurs. In all, this little dog with the strength of the bitch line through Kiwi of Dunkerque, has founded a splendid strain of under-11 lb Miniatures.

Ch. Cratloe Double Topping by Ch. Andyc Topper ex Cratloe Dream Topping. Owned and bred by Mrs Fountain.

·Mrs Bassett of the Merryweather Miniature Smooths had a bitch line in the mid-1950s bred from her Ch. Merryweather Magic ex Bumble Bee of Rowanhill. This little bitch was sired by another of the early imports, Delf von Vorgebirge. The Merryweathers can be found through Ch. Peredur Pimento and through him to Ch. Sinful Skinful. Mme de Bernes' lovely chocolate bitch, Ch. Rigol Phantom Phoebe, has a great-grandsire on the dam's side who is the grandsire of Ch. Pimento.

Mrs Fountain with the Cratloes has gradually climbed to the top awards. Her principal winner is Ch. Cratloe Double Topping: his sire is Ch. Andyc Topper, Ch. Bryn of Paxford ex Cumtru Threepenny Opera, and his dam Cratloe Gaynor, Cratloe Dream Topping by Ch. Topper. This dog has sired eight Champions.

5 Breeding

Breeding for top-flight Dachshunds cannot be achieved with purely pet stock. One MUST have a well-bred bitch who is also correctly constructed. It is easy enough to purchase a pup who owns a well-known sire or dam, though the litter from which she came may be far from typical. The novice should place himself in the hands of an expert on the particular variety he is interested in – explaining that the intention is to breed for show points. It is quite possible that the applicant's name will have to be put on a waiting list for such a puppy, but it is infinitely preferable to have the chance of good stock rather than rushing to purchase from the litter up the road.

In 1977 the Kennel Club in the U.K. brought in a regulation forbidding the matings of the different varieties, both in coat and size. If, however, a recessive should appear in a litter it is eligible for registration under the variety that it most closely resembles.

The ideal way to found a kennel (if one's purse permits) is to purchase a pair of litter sisters. The pedigree of these pups will contain the names of big-winning stock and they should carry the dominant characteristics for which this particular kennel is famous. The selection of these young hopefuls should be left to the breeder who will, of course, be familiar with the type of the puppies produced in the kennel. Dachshund puppies are notoriously difficult to assess, even to an expert of much experience, and a novice would find the task beyond his powers.

Having reared these bitches to maturity and perhaps having ventured into the show ring with varying degrees of success, the problem of their matings should have been planned well in advance, again with the help of the breeder who knows the background of their ancestors. They should be mated to different dogs who both carry the same name of one or more outstanding animals in the pedigree, this name or names also appearing in the bitch's pedigree.

It cannot be too strongly emphasised that the future success of a kennel depends very largely on the type of stock acquired as a foundation. Contrary to common belief, the dam is of the utmost importance in determining the type of puppies. A really excellent bitch who is also dominant for transmitting her own good points, even if mated to a second-rate dog, is far more valuable for the strength of a kennel, than is a not-so-good bitch mated to a top-flight dog.

The perfect Dachshund has yet to be produced, though during the last few years all varieties have seen more than one really outstanding animal; the aim of every breeder should be the production of individuals showing fewer or less obvious faults than their parents and therefore nearer to the ideal as repesented by the Standard of Points (see Chapter 11).

Having mated the litter sisters and reared the pups correctly, the help of their breeder or that of the owner of the sire should be enlisted when making the choice of which whelp to keep. It is not necessarily the largest puppy that one wants. The ideal pair to add to the novice's stock would be a dog from one litter, with a bitch from the second; the cousins ultimately being used for breeding.

Alternatively, it may be possible to persuade a breeder of repute to part with a young winning bitch – preferably a proved brood. Such an animal will prove more costly than the youngsters. In many cases this will be the better investment for the young ones may be difficult to mate, infertile or bad whelpers.

The older bitch may be mated in the same way that was planned for the young ones, i.e. an outstanding dog in her pedigree should be sought, or if no longer available, an immediate descendant.

Among the lay public, the idea persists that inbreeding (i.e. the mating of related individuals) is invariably attended by the production of weakly or mentally deficient offspring. Typical animals, which will consistently transmit their own good qualities to their progeny, can only be produced by intelligent breeding, and this means inbreeding. Type can only be fixed by breeding to a family line. A strain consists of a family of animals which can confidently be expected to transmit certain characteristics which have been concentrated in their physical and generative make-up by the mating through successive generations of individuals more or less nearly related. The more strongly a partner to a mating is inbred for a particular characteristic, the more likely it is to imprint that characteristic on its progeny. The danger of inbreeding is that it accentuates, or brings into prominence, faults as well as desirable characteristics. An inbred failing is as potent as is inbred quality, and in many ways more so. If in the course of breeding in this manner an objectionable fault appears frequently in the inbred stock, steps must be taken to cope with the danger of fixing these faults, by using a complete outcross, i.e. by introducing outside blood lines.

The degree to which it is safe or desirable to inbreed is a matter of opinion. In theory, there is no reason why unions between relatives should not be made, provided the relatives are known to be free from physical and mental weaknesses. For practical purposes, however, the inexperienced breeder will do well not to experiment in such close inbreeding as is involved in the mating of brother and sister, sire and daughter, or dam and son. These matings have been undertaken by breeders of long experience and with varying degrees of success. Unions between half-brother and half-sister, nephew and aunt, niece and uncle, and cousins of any degree of removal may be arranged with good results and without risk of deterioration of stamina in the progeny. Put briefly, line-breeding may be described as being the union of individuals belonging to the same main family in that they are eventually descended from the same ancestors. Line-breeding may be practised for many years in some strains without any close inbreeding and is a system which may be recommended to the inexperienced breeder.

In aiming for perfection, always breed to the Standard. If a subject to be mated is, for example, too high on the leg and shallow in keel, choose a partner that conforms to the requirements in anatomical formation, rather than one who is too exaggerated in these points. Some of the pups will resemble the correct parent, others the faulty one; if, however, one of the parents is overdone in brisket, a proportion of the pups will inherit this fault, and the resulting litter be almost worthless.

In breeding for colour, two basic principles should be borne in mind. The first is that weak pigmentation is often accompanied by constitutional weakness; the second that in breeding whole coloured, or self-coloured, individuals together there is a tendency for the progeny to be less strongly pigmented than their parents.

The original fount of pigmentation in the Dachshund as mentioned in the records of 1701, was 'from grey to black'. By 1848 the colour had become 'yellow or black with yellow extremities'. With the introduction of the blood of the Bavarian Bloodhound, and the various types of French Pointer who carried long drop-ears, the colour gradually changed to shades of red. All the other colour varieties – black and tan, brindle, and dapple – have derived from this and represent a weakening or dilution of the original pigment factors. If red is bred to red generation after generation, the colour becomes pale and washy, with light eyes, light nails and pink or brown noses; white markings appear on the chest or toes and general degeneration of the animal appears. If both parents to a union of this colour are deep in colour with dark eyes and black points the resulting progeny should not show any colour defects, though they may be lighter in colour than their parents. In breeding for reds, the deep cherry red, or the shaded red, in which the coat carries a certain amount of black, should be used as a partner to the golden or clear red, in preference to mating two goldens. The correct coloured mate for a golden is a black and tan. In the long-haired variety brindle represents the next step to black and tan, and may also strengthen the pigmentation of the reds. Two light-eyed

Dachshunds should never be mated together, for the incidence of this eye colour will prove dominant.

Chocolate is a tricky colour, and is probably a deviation from black and tan, caused by the loss, or repression, of a pigment factor. Chocolate should never be bred to red, such matings producing washy chocolates, or chocolatey reds, probably with pink noses or light eyes. It has been found that a red, even with completely dark points, if carrying chocolate in the pedigree, through the mating of a black and tan ancestor, in future litters may throw reds with chocolate noses – a most objectionable fault. Chocolate should only be mated to chocolate if both parents are really dark colour; mated to black and tan, the resulting pups will be deep-coloured black and tans or liver-coloured chocolates.

The dapple pattern emerged from the continuous mating of pale chocolates who had appeared in black and tan litters as a result of the repression of a pigment factor, these being even more lacking in pigment than light coloured chocolates, and upon which there were bluish grey blotches on a chocolate ground. Before this stage was reached, however, silver grey dogs appeared with loss of pigment in the eyes, resulting in the light yellow eye in the chocolates and the wall-eye or eyes of the dapple. There is a breeding rule that chocolates and dapples cannot be continued in pure breeding, they must be continuously crossed with the black and tan variety. The writer has seen litters resulting from the mating of two dapples (in both cases chocolates), in which more than 50 per cent of the whelps were white or largely white with the odd chocolate patches. In each case the whelps were blind or near blind, with small pink eyes. The mating of a chocolate dapple to a red produces a small proportion of red dapples; in this case the chocolate patches are on a red ground. The behaviour of the dapple coloration to reproduce itself cannot be relied upon, though it may appear in litters bred from a parent with only the smallest patch of colour. No dapple is recessive and cannot be looked for in litters unless one parent is of this colour. In other words this pattern is a dominant factor.

Two black and tans mated together will invariably produce only black and tan (this supposes there has been no near chocolate ancestor), red to red can give a proportion of black and tans as well as reds. There is the occasional dog or bitch who is dominant for the red gene and no matter which colour the partner may be, the resulting litter will be red.

The brindle colour to be found in the Long Hairs came about through the continuous mating of the early specimens of this variety, who were more yellow than red, to a dominant strain of black and tans. The red dogs so produced showed a sprinkling of black hairs here and there in the coat, possibly a black tail end, and a black line up the back with a black mask to the head. Brindle mated to black and tan will produce a majority of brindle, but will also contain reds and black and tans.

A bitch usually comes into season – that is, attains the physiological condition in which she can be mated – at regular intervals of six months. In the case of Dachshund bitches the six monthly period may be anything from eight months to even ten months between seasons but that is no cause for worry. The best time to mate a bitch of this breed is from the eleventh day of the start of the colour, until the thirteenth or even fourteenth day. Some animals, particularly in the Miniature varieties, are ready for mating earlier, maybe as early as the eighth day, although this is unusual. A young puppy may come into season at six months, though normally the age is nearer nine months. No Dachshund bitch should be mated on her first heat, maturity should be complete before subjecting the bitch to the strain of bearing, and in particular rearing, a litter. It is unwise to leave a bitch for a first litter later than four years and it is not essential that a bitch should have a litter. They are excellent mothers if given the opportunity, but will not suffer if this is not possible. Dachshund bitches are not alone in suffering from 'false pregnancies'; this is a condition which in some strains shows up approximately nine weeks after the season has terminated. The milk glands become engorged, the bitch takes a variety of the owner's personal belongings to her bed and becomes generally broody. The vet should be able to help disperse the milk and the owner can sponge the loaded glands with surgical spirit, or oil of Swallows (*see under* Aids For Well Being). Many vets suggest that the bitch who is liable to this condition should be mated at her next season. This will not prevent the glands filling after succeeding seasons, and the bitch develops an untidy underline.

All arrangements for the mating should have been made well in advance, the owner of the dog being agreeable to accepting the bitch and the stud fee having been notified to the owner. When colour is first observed the stud dog's owner should be advised, so that no other bitch should be taken to that dog on the particular day of the season, of bitch number one, when it is thought most suitable for the mating. A phone call to the stud dog's owner two days before the selected day can advise how the season is progressing, mention being made of the degree of 'colour' and whether the bitch is flirting with any other animal of the household. From this call it may be decided to postpone the mating day slightly – till the 'colour' is, as it should be, very pale and watery in appearance. Some bitches will stand to the dog for several days even when in full colour and puppies from such a mating may duly arrive. The ideal time for a natural mating is slightly later in a season than earlier. Some bitches who are made much of in their own homes are unwilling to accept a dog at any time; a good and capable stud dog will, however, achieve a mating if the owner of the bitch will steady her, the owner of the dog aiding the dog who will look for assistance to his master. A bitch when ready to stand to the dog shows her readiness by holding her tail to one side and should do this reflex action when introduced to the stud.

The owner of the bitch should clearly understand that the stud fee is for the dog's service, irrespective of whether a litter arrives. The majority of stud dog owners will offer a second service if no pups arrive. They must be notified immediately that the bitch has produced no litter on the expected day to complete the dog's record.

As most kennel owners now have adequate transport, the great majority of bitches for mating are brought to the dog, not sent by train. If the chosen dog is far afield and the train journey is necessary, the bitch should be sent some days in advance of the possible mating date so that she may become accustomed to her new surroundings and to what may be to her, strangers. For the novice owner who takes his bitch himself but is not familiar with the mating procedure, the two animals when introduced will probably appear not much interested. The bitch may growl and even attempt to snap at the dog. The dog will soon realise what she has come for and make advances. Should the bitch remain aggressive the dog's owner will probably suggest that the bitch has her jaws secured, to prevent his dog from being bitten. This does not hurt the bitch and gives the dog confidence. (A young inexperienced dog should not be used on a visiting bitch unless she is a proved matron and an easy subject, rather should such a dog mate a bitch who is known to him and he to her.) The dog will mount the bitch, and holding her tightly between his paws and legs, will insert the penis into her vagina and penetrate the cervix or aperture to the uterus. When in position the penis becomes engorged and is held in position by the contracting of the cervix, so causing a tie between the two. During this tie the dog is ejecting thousands of sperms, only some of which will become fertilised; this being governed by the number of ova that are ripe on that particular day in the bitch. With the tie still holding the dog will take his front legs off the bitch's back and gradually turn himself until he and she are back to back. This position may be held for anything up to forty minutes, when they will gradually slip apart. In a natural mating the two animals will play together and, with the bitch curling her tail to him, she will stand up to him with no help from the owners and a mating will be achieved. It is wise to steady the bitch throughout the tie, so causing no injury to the dog. A tie is not absolutely necessary for the production of a litter, the dog has merely to penetrate the cervix. A reliable stud will be ejaculating sperm as he achieves this position, with the sperm travelling up into the uterus.

After mating, the bitch may return home – care must be taken that she may not get access to a second stud dog, that day or the succeeding four or five. It is perfectly possible for a second mating between the bitch and the visitor to take place resulting in a litter of puppies by both sires. If the dog is of another coat variety this will show in the resulting litter, for he will have mated the bitch at the time of the ripening of additional ova supplementary to those ripe for the first or planned mating. It is not unknown to find a registration in the Kennel Gazette of a litter sired by 'Bold Baron or Red Duke'. This is interpreted to mean that the owners of both the dog and the bitch were not satisfied that the first mating had been completed and to make doubly sure had used another of the dogs in the kennel. In the case of mixed coats quite obviously this had not been planned.

The novice breeder must realise that though a planned mating for his bitch may have produced excellent puppies, some of whom may be winning in the ring, a second visit to the same stud may prove most disappointing for show points. The cause of this is that the genes in both dog and bitch have varied from those present at the time of the original mating and will, in fact, never be the same again. It is possible to mate the same two animals at three different seasons, with the stock getting progressively further from the Standard.

A method of finding the correct day for a successful mating is to purchase, from the chemist, Tes-Tape made by Lilly and Company or a similar product. When a bitch is ready to receive the dog she has eggs in the ovary and glucose is produced. At this time a test may be done; the Tes-Tape is put in the vagina, and if green spots appear on it this is a sure sign that the eggs are present.

One cause of bitches missing more than once is that they cannot relax away from their own homes. In these cases if the owner of the dog can be persuaded to take the dog to the bitch and serve her on her home ground, a litter should result. There are, of course, bitches who are infertile, and no matter which day is chosen to mate them, nothing results.

6 Infections in Bitches

Streptococci

The infection is present in bitches only. Its full name is 'Beta Haemolytic Streptococci', known as B.H.S.

Symptoms show themselves in three phases:
1 B.H.S. may cause sterility.
2 B.H.S. may cause abortion at mid-term.
3 B.H.S. may cause death of pups from 2–3 days of age. There is a gradual fading, resulting in death.

The bitch herself may develop toxaemia and succumb.

INFECTION
May be infected uterine discharge transferred from a bitch in season, or having whelped, when passing water, to the external genitals of the second bitch which squats at the same spot. The second possible method is for a sire to act as carrier. This infection is NOT a venereal disease. The sire may pick up the strep when servicing the infected bitch, and will carry the germs for approximately one week. If during this week he serves a clean bitch, he may infect her during the service. B.H.S. is not caused by the dog, but is *transferred* by him. The germ will have died, on the dog's genitals after a week to ten days.

TREATMENT
This is relatively simple, but if diagnosed after the pups begin to fade, is difficult, as the infection is transferred with the milk. The pups die of toxaemia and secondary enteritis from the dam's milk. It is necessary to remove the pups and either hand feed them, or use a foster mother. Pups and bitch should be treated with antibiotics. The strep causing the disease is not necessarily susceptible to the same drug each time; they show different reactions to Penicillin, Penicillin/Streptomycin and Chloromycetin. It is necessary to take a vaginal swab and then isolate the organism by running a sensitivity test, or, in the case of a dead pup, by conducting a post mortem, then a drug most likely to succeed may be chosen.

PREVENTION

It is most important to take every precaution against contracting the disease. Take a swab when the bitch is first in season (during the first 3–4 days) and have a sample analysed pathologically. If the strep is present, treat the bitch whilst in season, preferably before mating, although this can be done after the mating.

Take a swab again after whelping, or even, if worried, after the service. Owners of stud dogs may disinfect studs immediately after service; however, unless the correct disinfectant is used this could have bad results.

QUESTIONS AND ANSWERS

How long does a bitch carry the germ? Can any prophylactic action be taken as a precaution without taking swabs? 'Wogs' develop immunity towards any treatment. It is impossible to swab each and every bitch to see which antibiotic the wog is sensitive to. It can only be done when the bitch is in season. The organism is sensitive to rain and sunlight, but if left in protected areas it may have a life of up to two weeks; normally, in exposed areas, its life is from 7–10 days. It is only distributed by bitches in season, or just after mating.

It is preferred to run the bitches in season on concrete areas, which may be hosed and disinfected daily, rather than grass.

The bitch has to be treated to get rid of B.H.S. otherwise she will carry it to her dying day. The infection could be contracted on the first day of the bitch's season.

7 Whelping for the Novice

Reading one or two books on whelping does not, unfortunately, tell the novice all he or she should know; although of course it helps. Neither is whelping a case of leave-it-all-to-nature, or trust-to-luck. Our vets tell us that Dachshunds are notoriously bad whelpers, due probably to their shape, and that a number of bitches are lazy; but don't let this frighten you!

Having had your bitch mated, you now settle back to wait, with dreams of a lovely litter. During pregnancy the bitch should lead a normal life with the usual amount of exercise. Diet is also important but provided the diet is adequate in protein, vitamins and minerals, with a little carbohydrate added, no additions are required until the bitch shows obvious signs of being in whelp. After that an increase in food is essential; for example, give milk for breakfast, $\frac{1}{2}$ lb fish at midday, and $\frac{3}{4}$ lb raw meat at supper time; include 10 Vetzymes, 1 teaspoon of Stress, $\frac{1}{4}$ teaspoon of cod liver oil, with the amount of carbohydrate depending on the fatness of the bitch (these amounts refer to Standard Dachshunds).

About a week before the sixty-third day, the bitch should be settled in her whelping quarters. If she is a kennel dog, bring her preferably into the house so that she will be under close observation and because at this time, more than ever, the bitch appreciates the extra attention and affection. Above all one can then watch every sign of the coming labour. One's greatest asset at this time is the power of observation. The whelping box should be long enough for the bitch to lie full length and wide enough for her and, say, six pups to spread out and 'bask' under the infra-red lamp. (No pet basket please.) See also that the room is really warm as the bitch loses a lot of heat and energy and easily becomes chilled during whelping. Newspaper should be spread thickly in the box so that the bed can be changed frequently, but there should never be blankets.

Usually a bitch whelps any time from the fifty-ninth day, so be on the look out. She becomes unsettled and uneasy, pants a lot and cries, and probably refuses food twenty-four hours before the puppies arrive. Having scratched up all her bedding and possibly torn up a lot more, the bitch then settles down quietly to await the mechanism which starts the puppy along the birth canal. It is impossible to mistake the muscular

tension which induces the bitch to heave and so push the puppy out –
her body from her shoulders to her tail is exerted. This first heave,
usually accompanied by a cry from the bitch, is the most important
part of whelping – take NOTE of the time.

Any time after this, if the bitch continues to labour, a puppy should
arrive, head or tail first is of no importance. With a maiden bitch she
is often too bewildered over her first two or three whelps to be able to
cope with them, and this can also happen if she is very big. As a rule
the puppy is born in an opaque bag which contains fluid; tear the bag
open and wipe the puppy's mouth and nostrils dry – most important
this, as the whelp can quickly drown in this fluid if both bitch and
owner just look on and wonder 'what next'!

Now the cord; if the bitch does not attend to this, pinch the cord
about $1\frac{1}{2}$ inches from the whelp's abdomen, and then cut through this
area. Now the bitch should lick the puppy and nuzzle it to her – a
strong whelp finds a nipple on its own and starts to suck. If the bitch
couldn't care less or objects, then dry the pup properly and put it on
a well covered and warm hot-water bottle. The after-birth and soiled
bedding should be removed after each birth. Now a succession of pups
should arrive with intervals of five minutes or two hours between each.
As the whelping progresses and more pups arrive the bitch will want
her offspring with her, also they will be ready for their first feed, so
any pups that have been taken away should now be returned to her.
During whelping some bitches appreciate warm milk with a little
glucose added; give her as much of this as she wants.

When you are sure that whelping has finished, and having fore-
warned him that you have a bitch whelping, ask your vet to come and
examine her for either retained placenta or puppy. This visit is worth
so much; puppies can be smothered by a fidgety bitch who is not happy
within herself, or septicaemia can start, which can mean goodbye to
milk, to puppies, and to the bitch.

As soon as all is well take the bitch outside for toilet (she may need
coaxing out during the succeeding days), then put a clean blanket in
her box, either nailed on to the floor, or spread over a false floor and
then fitted in. Now take the infra-red lamp and put it the distance from
the puppies which just keeps them warm, because infra-red rays are of
such a frequency as to penetrate the body and thus give internal
warmth. I have found a 250 watt lamp dull-emitter is adequate; testing
with one's hand soon ascertains the correct distance that the lamp
should be suspended overhead.

In place of a blanket in the whelping box a *vet bed* may be found
satisfactory. I was delighted to be introduced to one; the whelps are
kept warm and clean and, with a spare *vet bed*, a change can be made
when needed (I used newspaper as well, under the *vet bed*); also the

pups can move around freely on this without slipping, so their hind-quarters develop well.

removeable pigrail – 2 inches wide

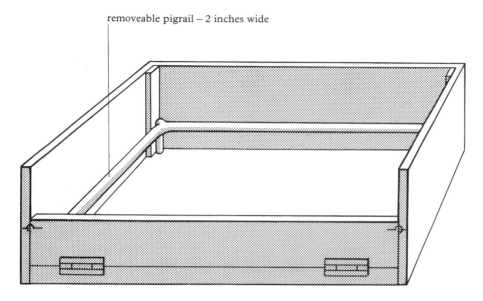

FIGURE 1:
Whelping box

When the pups are four days old any dew-claws on hind legs must be removed. It is probably better for a novice to get a knowledgeable friend or the veterinary surgeon to remove dew-claws from a first litter. The operation should be watched carefully for future reference. It is easily and quickly done if someone is there to hold the puppies. The breeder with little experience will soon find the technique of doing it single handed. A pair of blunt-pointed, preferably short-bladed, scissors are needed, with a few small wads of cotton wool or lint and a styptic to stop the bleeding. Tincture of perchloride of iron, or Friar's Balsam are quite satisfactory.

The puppy should be held facing the operator, with the hindlegs held out towards him. He must hold the leg gently but firmly with the left hand, spreading the dew-claw slightly away from the leg, while with the right hand he places the open blades of the scissors flush with the leg, with the dew-claw between the blades; the blades being as close as possible to the leg and parallel with it. A single closing of the scissor blades removes the entire digit at the joint. It is essential to remove it in this way, for if a small piece of bone is left it will grow and be unsightly as well as troublesome. Many puppies hardly notice this operation, some may give a single cry, but it appears almost painless at this age. Any bleeding should be stopped by pressure with a pad moistened with the particular styptic chosen. The second claw (if present) should then be taken off and the pup returned to its bed. The bitch, if an anxious type, should have been removed well out of earshot before starting the task. The puppies should be checked over to be sure that no dew-claw has been missed and that all bleeding has stopped. The bitch can then be allowed to return to her family and will notice nothing amiss.

For the bitch my choice of diet is milk, glucose and *Farex* for the first twenty-four hours after whelping; then egg and milk, plenty of fish and milk pudding, until, after forty-eight hours, the bitch is back to meat. According to the number of pups and the size of the bitch, the diet varies, but I prefer to feed the bitch as she looks – basically 1 qt milk, $1\frac{1}{2}$ lb raw or cooked meat, also carbohydrate; she gets the essential vitamins and minerals in 10 Vetzyme, 2 teaspoons of Stress and 1 teaspoon of cod liver oil. My bitches always leave a family looking very fit and blooming. In fact, I would be very concerned if they did not maintain such a condition, meat, milk, fish, carbohydrate and the essential supplements, i.e. vitamins and minerals, having been given as to the bitch's needs. Like a cow, a bitch cannot produce sufficient milk if she is not fed on a maintenance diet plus the extra food necessary to produce the amount required by each puppy.

THE COMPLICATIONS OF WHELPING

A word first about PITUITRIN. Most people know of pituitrin and some people have the idea that it can be given *ad lib* during whelping. Only under strict veterinary supervision can this be given and only a very little then. Although a useful drug it is not to be relied upon to produce results as if by some form of magic.

During whelping there may well be occasions when it is necessary to call in the vet. These occasions are:

1 If there is a green, dark discharge either during or before whelping. This usually means a dead whelp – a whitish discharge during whelping is normal.
2 If the bedding appears *very wet* with colourless, odourless fluid – as distinct from urine – and the bitch just sits looking bewildered. This is usually a case of 'the water breaking' followed by uterine inertia.
3 If the bitch, having started to whelp normally, produces one or two pups easily and then stops. This is once again uterine inertia.
4 If two hours have elapsed since the bitch was first noticed to heave and regular labouring has continued during that time but no whelps have arrived, then advice must be sought – this is where my point about noting the time comes in. Furthermore, attention must be paid that no more than two hours should elapse *between* the birth of one puppy and the next without seeking advice.
5 If there is an incorrect presentation of the whelp and the pup is fixed by a foot, head, or any part being out of position and therefore

catching on the brim, then assistance is urgently required, for the bitch will quickly become exhausted.

6 If the sixty-third day comes and goes and there is no sign of whelping there is no need for concern provided the bitch looks well and is eating properly; but on the sixty-sixth day – so long as the dates are correct – treatment from the vet must then be *insisted* upon in order to preserve the lives of bitch and whelps.

7 If the bitch shows signs of hysterical excitement and is panting continuously, then the puppies must be taken away from the bitch and the vet must be sent for *at once*. These symptoms indicate eclampsia, or calcium collapse, which is due to the bitch giving too generously to her puppies of her own store of calcium. In these days of well-fed and well-cared-for bitches this rarely happens but if it does occur then veterinary help *must* be *speedily* obtained.

8 If the milk glands harden, then the vet's guidance will have to be sought. This may occur either before, or immediately after, whelping, and a careful watch should be kept to see that there is no inflammation present to cause the hardening.

At all times, if one is not a good judge as to when an animal is slightly 'off colour', then the thermometer must be relied upon. It is advisable to check the bitch's temperature for three days after whelping in case of Metritis. Although the temperature is normally raised a little after whelping, anything from 103° upwards is a danger signal.

Here I would like to add that when puppies are about two weeks old it is advisable to feel the length of their front claws; these are usually like needle points, and can soon begin to scratch the poor bitch continually; they must be *cut* – taking *great care* as you do it.

Ears are of vital importance – keep these very clean. There is no excuse for having puppies with dirty ears (and so many are sold in this condition too!). We use a specially-prepared powder which is very reliable, and which can be obtained from any chemist.

A Plea or Advice

I have been appalled by the deaths of perfectly healthy bitches (of different breeds) following abdominal operations, either from spaying of pets or from Caesarean section. I wonder very much why this has to happen, and if the answer is a very human one – the dog needs its owner at the moment it comes out of the anaesthetic. Surely we are all sensible enough to care for our dogs even if it necessitates sitting up all night until the animal is really conscious and helping when he struggles, for struggle he will, to get away from the thing that is hurting in his inside.

I know of many different cases of the above when the operation has ended in tragedy and each time the animal has been taken from its home by the vet to his surgery. Meanwhile the owner has all faith in what is about to happen to his animal. Invariably death comes after the operation, and, on enquiry, one is told that it is due to shock or pneumonia from the anaesthesia. I think the answer to the above cases could lie in the post-operative care.

The owner should always remember to take the dog to the surgery *when* the vet is ready to operate and *not* let it be carted off by him when he calls and then left in the surgery wondering what is going to happen to it. Again, after the operation, the animal should not be left at the vet's surgery to struggle, in a semi-conscious state, searching for home and master, but immediately taken home wrapped in a warm blanket.

The after-care of operation cases is simple. At first, in the semi-conscious state, warmth is vital; this means a warm room, or a heater in the kennel, not just several hot-water bottles! At the same time it is essential to maintain a clear airway by drawing the tongue out between the teeth at the side of the mouth. A bitch with newborn pups will usually settle when her pups start to suck and neither she nor the puppies will worry about the incision. Should she be the exception, then there is no alternative but to put a wide roll of cardboard around her neck *à-la-mode* of the giraffe women.

Fluids with glucose are a necessity as soon as the dog desires to drink; after that, unless otherwise ordered by the vet, give an egg in milk; in a few hours regular feeding can commence with a light high-protein diet followed by a gradual return to a normal diet if all is going well. Should the animal refuse to eat or drink, and persist in doing so, raw liver is the easiest to 'push down'. Fluid can always be set in a firm jelly with gelatine and small pieces also 'pushed down'. This method is far more reliable than pouring fluid down the animal's throat, thus running the risk of it going into the lungs.

All through this nursing after surgery a check should be kept on the dog's temperature. 101.4 is the normal temperature for a dog.

8 Puppy Rearing

The successful rearing of Dachshund puppies calls for much care and not a little skill. The Teckel is not a delicate breed yet it must be admitted that a large proportion of puppies, born of illustrious parents, go wrong through the carelessness, or ignorance, of their owners. It must be understood that each breeder must bring into consideration, intelligence, sympathy and affection for youngsters, if success is to be achieved. Each puppy must be treated as an individual and have its own ration of daily fussing from an early age, for then it will develop confidence in its owner and reward him with much affection.

All puppies are born with their eyes closed and sealed, likewise the ears, and these will not usually open before the twelfth day. When new-born the whelps often appear quite different in colour from what they will be as adults. The black and tans remain the same with the tan deepening in colour as they get older. In Smooths, red pups may first look sooty black, but quickly begin to lighten. In the Long Hairs, the reds are much darker, almost dirty grey, those which are to be shaded reds look almost black, but if the hair is turned back a brownish hue will be noticed at the roots. Clear reds may show quite a lot of black, particularly on the top of the head and along the line of the back. If a puppy is going to turn out black and tan the hair on the body will be black to the roots and its skin blue. Similar remarks apply to the wire-haired variety. Here the usual colours are somewhat different to those commonly seen in Smooths and Long Hairs. The pepper and salt, or grizzle colour of the adults is often preceded by a blue and tan, or very dark, appearance in the puppy and a youngster that is born a grizzle may finish up a clear red.

Dachshund bitches are as a rule fairly prolific. The average number of pups in a litter is five, though as many as ten may be born. If a large family is expected the owner must prepare to help with the feeding.

In the previous chapter the care of the whelping bitch was dealt with, and now we come to the important time when the puppies need weaning. Now this does not mean waiting until the bitch is ready to leave her litter, but should take place at three weeks of age, unless the litter is a small one (three or under); then wait until they are a month old. The puppies should firstly be taught to lap – this they will learn quite readily if held and the milk mixture gently put to their mouths; with a little encouragement and a little patience the youngsters will soon start feeding and become independent.

Before giving the diet usually fed to puppies, we must consider what *is* an adequate diet, and the following are the essential items. This is given here so as to provide the knowledge and understanding of food necessary to keep a dog in good health.

Protein foods: meat, rabbit, cheese, liver, sheep's head, eggs – all foods of animal origin, vital for the growth of the dog's whole body.

Carbohydrates: found in wholemeal biscuits; this supplies muscle, energy and warmth.

Vitamins and minerals: these must be considered and included.

Vitamin A: found in milk, animal fat, cod and halibut liver oil, and necessary for growth in the young.

Vitamin B: found in wholemeal cereals, eggs and yeast; one of the easiest sources of Vetzymes; vital for the nervous system and general good health.

Vitamin C: found in fruit – most dogs like fruit and rosehip syrup can be given to puppies for pure blood.

Vitamin D: found in cod or halibut liver oil – the sunshine vitamin; vital for growth and strong, sound bone.

Vitamin E: found in wheat germ, oil, meat and eggs. The fertility vitamin.

Vitamin F: found in milk and eggs, and essential for healthy skin.

Minerals: calcium, phosphorus and iron are covered by Vetzyme and Stress, and should be given as directed.

THE TYPE OF MILK

Most breeders have their own ideas about which type of milk to use. I prefer full cream Jersey milk to which has been added one egg yolk to a pint. Ostermilk No. 2 made up as directed for baby feeding, makes a good alternative.

Farex: without doubt the best combination is as follows:

1 Pkt Farex	1 Pkt Complan
1 Pkt Farlene	1 Pkt Glucose

all mixed well together; this really does give baby puppies a good start in weaning.

HANDREARING VERY YOUNG WHELPS

There are two methods for doing this, both using a premature Feeder, which may be purchased from the chemists, John Bell and Croydon in Wigmore Street, London. The first way is to feed four-hourly using a mixture of Channel Island milk (1 breakfast cupful) $\frac{1}{2}$ pint, 2 teaspoons of *Glucodin* and 1 tablespoon of evaporated milk. Mix cold, then warm to blood heat, and use as required.

The second method is to feed five times during the day, and once at night. The mixture in this case being Ostermilk No. 2 1 level table-spoon, 1 dessertspoon of Glucodin, 3 oz of boiled water, and one drop of Adexolin for each pup. In both cases scraped raw meat should be added at the end of a fortnight.

After each feed puppies must be persuaded to urinate and evacuate by using cotton wool wrung out in warm water and applied with a light touch to simulate the tongue of the bitch.

DIET – FOR A STANDARD DACHSHUND PUPPY

3rd to 4th week: now is the time to start the puppy on fresh raw meat, scraped best beef, about the size of a walnut, twice during the day.

4th to 5th week: 2 oz warm milk with a dessertspoonful of Farex mixture (as mentioned above) three times during the day; give 1 oz finely minced raw beef twice during the day. Pups can be wormed under veterinary advice.

5th to 6th week: 7.30 a.m. scrambled egg, add a dessertspoonful of Lowe's Wholemilk puppy food and mix together. (If you do this whilst egg is hot there should be suffcient moisture to soften the biscuits adequately).
11 a.m. 2 oz warm milk with Farex.
2 p.m. 2 oz minced raw meat.
5 p.m. 2 oz warm milk with Farex.
9 p.m. 2 oz minced raw meat, add one Vetzyme tablet, saltspoonful of Stress, one halibut liver oil capsule.

Puppies do vary considerably in the amounts they will or can consume at this age, especially as some dams regurgitate their food for their whelps. From the 6th week onwards the dam should be away from her puppies: progress with their diet needs concentration.

6th to 12th week: feed as above, but:
1 Increase meat gradually to 8 oz per day and use small pieces in place of mince.
2 Introduce Wilson Meal's, a tablespoonful, and moisten with gravy.
3 Give Vetzyme and Stress in amounts recommended by the makers.

3rd to 4th months: 7.30 a.m. 4 oz lightly cooked meat, a handful of Lowe's Carta Carna puppy food, and a handful of Wilson's, all slightly moistened with gravy.
1 p.m. 4 oz warm milk, add level tablespoonful of Farex mixture.
6 p.m. 6 oz raw meat, add Vetzyme, Stress and halibut liver oil capsules.
8.30 p.m. 2 oz warm milk.

5th to 6th months: continue with the three main meals per day as given above, omit last milk feed. Here a little discretion is required as to quantity of milk and biscuit given; if the puppy is over fat, a little less; if thin, extra milk and biscuit.

6th to 12th months: at this stage three meals per day are usually adequate and I give a meat meal first thing.
7.30 a.m. 4 oz cooked meat mixed with a quantity (governed by figure) of biscuit, also a handful of Wilson's Meal.
Noon $\frac{1}{4}$ pint milk – with or without Farex mixture.
6.30 p.m. 6–8 oz raw meat, with Vetzyme and Stress given in quantities as directed and $\frac{1}{4}$ teaspoonful of cod liver oil.

If the youngster is well grown by twelve months, feed meat and Wilson's Meal and biscuits – 12 oz meat – all together in the evening. Give a milky breakfast, approximately $\frac{1}{4}$ pint milk and a few dry biscuits.

FEEDING FOR A MINIATURE DACHSHUND PUPPY
Half the amounts as for a standard.

3rd to 4th week: fresh raw meat – best beef, scraped $\frac{1}{2}$ teaspoon; *OR* brains from a sheep's head – mash these and add some gravy from the cooking – give 1 teaspoonful (BUT take great care there are no bone splinters in the brain); feed twice during the day.

4th to 5th week: 1 tablespoon of warm milk and a level teaspoon of Farex mixture three times daily. Give a teaspoonful of finely-minced raw beef twice during the day. If necessary pups can be wormed under veterinary advice.

5th to 6th week: *7.30 a.m.* $\frac{1}{2}$ a scrambled egg and $\frac{1}{2}$ Farley's rusk, in small pieces, mixed lightly together.
11 a.m. 1 oz warm milk, heaped teaspoon of Farex mixture.
2 p.m. dessertspoon of meat either minced, or, at this stage, cut into small pieces.
5 p.m. as 11 a.m.
9 p.m. meat as at 2 p.m., add $\frac{1}{2}$ Vetzyme, $\frac{1}{2}$ saltspoon of Stress and 1 halibut liver oil capsule.

Puppies do vary considerably in amounts they will or can consume at this age, especially as some dams regurgitate their food for their whelps. From the 6th week onwards the dam should be away from her puppies, and then getting them on with their diet really needs concentrating upon. One of the easiest ways of knowing how food suits a puppy is by watching day by day progress *without* any upset tummies. Diarrhoea *usually* means too much, or too rich, food (persistent diarrhoea usually means infection.) Large amounts of food at long intervals make for pot belly and rib cage showing. A well-fed and well-nourished puppy should look well-rounded with adequate bone.

6th to 12th week: please revert to amounts for a Standard but give half all amounts.

METRIC CONVERSION TABLE

	IMPERIAL	METRIC
weight	1 oz	25 g (grammes)
	2 oz	50 g
	4 oz	100 g
	8 oz	225 g
capacity	$\frac{1}{4}$ pt	150 ml (millilitres)
	$\frac{1}{2}$ pt	300 ml
	1 pt	600 ml
	1 tsp	5 ml
	1 dsp	10 ml
	1 tbs	15 ml

This is the type of diet that can be continued as the dog grows, but condition must govern quantities. Also, do remember that a dog that is housed comfortably with a warm bed utilises its food intake to a greater advantage than a poorly-housed dog. The latter will be using the food only to keep itself warm, and so growth will become retarded.

'DON'TS'
Never overfeed, and remember that a dog has a small stomach with strong gastric juices which deal quickly with food.

Puppies should not be over fat or skinny but nicely covered.

Never feed sloppy or wet meals – this upsets the digestion; biscuits should be fed slightly moistened with good meat stock, the resulting consistency being dry and crumbly.

Feed at regular times whenever possible.

Never give meat straight from a refrigerator.

Never leave food uneaten – pick up the dish.

EXERCISE
The happiest puppies are those which are allowed freedom for their exercise; it is surprising that they never wander away. If given such liberty, it must be remembered not to let the puppies racket about too much and so become overtired.

To conclude: In the latter part of the weaning stages, the dam has been taken away from her family for varying lengths of time, daily. In any case, facilities must be available in their quarters for the dam to get out of reach of her puppies. By eight weeks of age she has usually finished with them, except for the occasional game. If a romp precedes each meal, the fully-fed puppies will be content to retire to their sleeping box, whereas if they are shut up in a small kennel throughout the day they will get bored, sit about and become noisy. Constant close confinement, too, may cause them to become nervous, shy, and stupid.

A child's playpen that can be moved from place to place in the garden during fine weather is a useful adjunct to the nursery equipment. The mental health of young stock is as important as physical well-being. The great thing is to keep the pups happy, interested in life and mentally alert and this can best be effected by giving them opportunities to experience new sensations and so gather varied mental impressions. Up to the age of two months or so Dachshunds must not be allowed to be too much on their feet. Play and exercise are of course, essential, but never let them get overtired. Immediately their romping flags, put them to bed. They will soon settle down for sleep.

As they grow in strength they will show a tendency to dig in any soft soil that they discover. This is a perfectly natural form of exercise and should not be discouraged. If the whelps have been well reared no harm will result from their delving – though it may well spoil the appearance of your garden. Jumping and climbing must, however, be prevented and if kept in the house puppies must not be allowed to ascend or descend the stairs, or for that matter climb on to the chairs. These matters are really important, as leaping or tumbling even from a small height will ruin their fronts and feet. A puppy's shoulder muscles are too easily overstretched with violent exertions and this will not tighten sufficiently with age, giving what is known as 'out at elbows appearance' and so debarring your young hopeful from the show ring. Try to keep the puppies plump, but not unduly fat. A whelp that is too corpulent is likely to go unsound by reason of the excessive weight its infantile legs and feet are called upon to bear.

A well-managed litter which has been carefully dosed for worms, may show the signs of worm infestation again at around four months of age. An infested puppy shows signs of this with a staring coat, diarrheoa and the passage of the occasional worm. Another early sign is the tendency to develop a pot belly after feeding; the presence of slimy mucous in the motions is usually the first sign, with slowing up of progress. A standstill in weight will follow unless the worms are removed.

Expert advice should always be sought from the veterinary surgeon when puppies need worming. The best and most effective remedies cannot be bought over the counter at the chemist, they must be obtained from the professional man and instructions must be faithfully observed. Modern remedies are a great advance on the more old fashioned and one gain is that fasting need not be observed. The medicine is usually given in tablet form. The puppy should be held on a table, the tablet slipped to the very back of the tongue and the mouth closed, at the same time the throat should be rubbed very gently downwards. If the tablet is placed too far forward the puppy will merely spit it out. Some puppies are very clever at holding the tablet in the mouth until put down and then getting rid of it, and it is not easy to decide just which of the litter has lost its dose.

It is wise to keep an eye on the litter for an hour or so in case of vomiting which may occur and lead to the same problem; plenty of warning is usually given before a puppy vomits; it should be picked up at once and the mouth held firmly shut. Any regurgitated matter will then have to be swallowed again.

With a heavy infestation worms may be passed for twenty-four hours and it is wise to repeat the dose in a fortnight's time.

Buyers of eight-week-old puppies should be told of the great importance of vaccination against the virus diseases of Distemper (which includes Hardpad disease) and Canine Virus Hepatitis; also of Leptospiral Jaundice which is due to another kind of organism. These can now be combined into a single inoculation. Most veterinary surgeons now vaccinate at nine to ten weeks with a booster dose a year later. The results are most satisfactory and no prejudice due to lack of knowledge or unwillingness to face the facts, should be allowed to stand in the way of this protection to animals which cannot help themselves. Unfortunately there is the occasional animal who does not react to the inoculation and, if the booster dose is not given, will most surely meet, at some stage during his lifetime, with one of these viruses and all veterinary help at that time may be of no avail.

However good its inheritance may be, hereditary potentialities cannot be fulfilled in any puppy unless its environment, in the widest sense of the word, is favourable. A good environment in the case of puppies is one in which the dam is a sensible and devoted mother; the feeding throughout is such as to provide all the ingredients of a correct diet, giving adequate nourishment for the growing body with all its needs; freedom and room to play, with the exercise that involves, are ensured; and relations between the puppies and humans are those of affection and understanding.

By the time the puppies have reached the age of two or three months the novice breeder will certainly be anxious to reduce the number, but fearful of selling the best and finding that his choice is faulty. This problem, and in the Dachshund this *is* a problem, is not an easy one to solve. The selection of Dachshund puppies at under six months is a gamble. The pick of the litter at twelve weeks, may, by the time it has reached eight months, be just a charming pet with no Show potentialities. The backward whelp may well outstrip the litter mates, developing into a really promising Show proposition. The best of the pups should be 'run on' and, with time, will separate themselves into bad, good, or very good.

To assess the puppies, when ready to part with the least attractive, each pup should be examined carefully. The chest should be broad and the ribbing well sprung outwards. A narrow chest will always be this. The body should be long, the legs short, with heavy bone in proportion to the size. The back should be level, and the hind-quarters broad. The top of the shoulder blade should be felt with the fingers and an imaginary line dopped from this position to the table on which the puppy is standing. If this plumb-line falls behind the feet, the position of the shoulders is correct; if it falls in front of the feet the shoulders are upright and will never improve. The line may fall midway through the feet and this again is incorrect, showing that the shoulders are not sufficiently angulated. The feet should be compact and if the puppy has been on hard ground for some part of each day, the nails should be short and showing no hooks on any nail. Several of the puppies may be equally good in the points one is looking for, so this is where the tightest elbows and the best heads will be searched for. The mouths of the selected pups must be examined and if there is any bite but a scissor (the back of the top teeth resting easily on the front of the lowers), the whelp must be discarded. The best pups should show breadth of chest, length of body, width behind, short legs and compact feet. The depth of chest will develop with age, an overdeveloped depth in a young pup may well be the ugly fault of a steep keel. This at maturity shows the underline to be short, finishing abruptly without the gently sweeping upward curve which is essential for a Dachshund in the show ring.

Most experienced breeders hold views on the best age at which to assess the future prospect of a puppy. Some hold that it is quite possible to pick a puppy shortly after birth. Others at three weeks or so, whilst another breeder can decide at eight weeks. There is almost unanimous agreement that if it is possible to run on the whole litter till at least six months the choice is then easy, the good having left the poor well behind.

The novice breeder should understand that puppies vary within very wide limits in the rate at which they 'make up' or develop. In certain strains the youngsters appear to be perfectly mature at a year, whilst the offspring of other strains remain immature and raw until well into their second year. Bitches often develop more quickly than dogs. The young dogs frequently refusing food and fretting should be checked in their development by contact with bitches in season. A Dachshund possessing great length and that extra look of refinement or quality may remain rather shallow in brisket until eighteen months or so, when it may let down and tighten all round, ending up as an outstandingly good specimen. Late developers usually prove to be good lasters until five or more years, retaining their quality long after the 'flash in the pan' youngster has faded out.

The novice must realise that the selection of a Dachshund puppy from the nest is always in some degree a gamble for good or bad. Even the expert can pick a dud. The old rule-of-thumb method of choosing the biggest puppy, with the biggest head and heaviest bone has nothing to recommend it. It can be a most unreliable guide and very often results in the selector being left with the largest, coarsest, and least sound member of the litter.

The subject of correct movement of the Dachshund is tricky and open to a wide range of variations. What to one breeder is good, is to another anathema. The correct articulation of the pelvis to the spine (30°) coupled with a right-angle formation of the femur to the stifle joint, with almost horizontal tibia and fibula to the hock joint, and the perpendicular foot bones, is good or bad depending upon the angulation and length of bones involved. Added to this, muscles, which are connected to the bones by tendons across the joints, have much stronger pull where the range of muscle movement is not exaggerated. The correct angled pelvis and the not too long bones go to make a strong structure, and the dog moves quickly and easily with a real push from the hind feet. Far too many move with effort, with back legs under the body and feet almost touching the stomach. This is wrong for a working dog.

9 Training

In training a puppy to the lead, never let it pull, and if it shows an inclination to drag along the ground, take the collar (a light narrow one) and lead off, and return it to its box for that day. Many small pups do not take kindly to a collar, consequently one must only put this on for a short while daily. The next step is to attach a light lead and induce the puppy to follow. Again this may be difficult, if so, attach a length of string to the collar and from time to time take this lightly in the hand and call the puppy to you. The determined puppy may take many weeks to move with one, but on no account must the owner lose patience and scold the pup; rather stop trying for that day. These first steps in lead training should be in the garden.

The day will come when the pup is ready to go out amongst the traffic, and it is often the wisest plan to carry the puppy for a short distance merely to let it see and hear the cars. Anything as small as a Dachshund can be very intimidated by the rush of the passing traffic. Having gained the pup's confidence, induce it to take a short walk, possibly ten minutes daily, gradually increasing as and when it seems willing. No puppy should be taken for walks till quite four and half to five months, and then only short distances, say half a mile daily.

As the puppy grows it may well be necessary for the owner to scold it, on no occasion should it be thrashed. The breed being extraordinarily sensitive, severe punishment or a blow could permanently cow or sour the pupil's temperament. The puppy will, or should be, relying upon its owner for food and affection, so all that is necessary will be an admonition by the tone of voice.

A youngster who is destined for the show ring, must have experience of all manner of sounds, and of the crowds such as can be found in Woolworth's. Car riding can upset some, so this should be gradually introduced. If there is sickness, the vet will supply the correct treatment. In the ring a raw puppy who is used to all manner of strange sounds and surfaces which it has walked on, and who has been given the chance to meet strangers, and be handled by them, will make the very best of its chances during the short while it is under the judicial eyes. A shy puppy, no matter how correct in construction, is unable to catch the judge's eye. The judge of the day can only place the exhibits who are not only well-made but also have the ability to show this with happy deportment.

If the owner of the young hopeful makes enquiries around amongst friends and acquaintances, he will probably hear of the local canine association which, quite probably, may be sponsoring 'Ringcraft' classes for its members. These classes are for puppies and for unruly dogs whose owners have let them get out of control. The puppy will have a chance to mix with other varieties, and be taught the show procedure. This is by no means difficult for the owner or the puppy. All show prospects must be taught to walk on a loose lead on the owner's left hand side; to stop, and to stand to attention when ordered; to stand on a table, and to tolerate handling by a complete stranger. The handling involves the examination of the teeth, touching the dog, and running the hands down the shoulders, feeling the feet, and possibly re-standing the dog. The correct stance should show the dog at full stretch (but not exaggerated), the head up, and the front feet well placed under the body. Home lessons (if no 'Ringcraft' classes available) should be started with possibly ten minutes instruction daily, amongst the exercises should be that of stand to attention for about two minutes, with rewards being given when this is mastered. Each time the pup moves he should be told to stand, and maybe a leg should be put into position, each time repeating the order 'stand'. The best tit-bit, and one much enjoyed, is well-boiled liver cut into dice-shaped portions; for the show ring this is easy to handle. Another favourite dainty is cheese, also diced.

10 Character

The Dachshund is first and foremost a sporting dog, and in the country of its origin is still considered as such. The foresters use their dogs for tracking, not only for fox and hare, but also for wounded deer, and, in the thick forest, for the sauhatz or wild boar. The Dachshund on account of its low stature and great courage and persistence in following a scent, is fitted for this task; the boar's tusks being a dangerous weapon to any dog who cannot move smartly.

The Germans rate this hunting ability highly, consequently all their dogs are considerably lighter in weight and higher on the leg than those we are familiar with in England and in the U.S.A. They must carry good round bone, and in the case of the Long Hairs, have a flat coat, though not so profuse as that seen in England.

The hunting ability has been bred into the Dachshund from its earliest inception, and those of today who unfortunately spend too much time as pampered pets, would, if given the chance, disappear down a hole in the wood to the consternation of the owner.

In the immediate post-war years of 1946 and onwards, Colonel Phipps, who had previously been the owner of the then famous Talavera prefix in Smooth Fox Terriers, became a Dachshund devotee. He was at one time Master of the North Northumberland Foxhounds, and instead of a hunt terrier used Dachshunds for the purpose of going to ground for the fox. He found these dogs quite excellent, and never returned to the use of a terrier.

Many are the stories of Smooth and Wire Dachshunds working below ground for hours. The writer knows well the strain that this can cause on the owner, particularly if the dog has not been seen to enter, for in a large area of woodland there are many underground entrances and only by luck can the dog be heard giving tongue below the surface. In one known instance, a bitch did not return; twelve hours later she was located by hearing a muffled bark; come she would not. Digging started and she was found to be trapped by a root. In another story, again a bitch went to ground, and was not seen for four days, this time she got out, very dirty, very thirsty, and very excited.

'For the forester his Dachshund must be able to track the shot game, holding the opinion that the spotsman's most binding rule is to spare game suffering. The modern excellence of the gun, has more or less the ascendancy over game, unless the deer is shot in the belly or legs.

In this case it must endure severe pain for hours. The Dachshund through Bracke-heredity (tracking) is endowed with many qualities which make him naturally suited to this type of work. He has a superlatively good nose, and as he is short-legged can keep his nose down continuously. Thanks to his short legs he is not too speedy, and thus does not so easily overrun the scent. His drop ears keep noise and disturbing sounds at a distance, and so he can concentrate completely on his nose work.'

The preceding paragraph has been taken from the work of Dr Schneider Leyer, and to quote further from this: 'The goal at which the Dachshund breeder must aim is the preservation of the working Dachshund according to the guidance of our fathers and forefathers. His good qualities, such as hatred of vermin, combined with sharpness, intelligence and courage, fine nose, passion for hunting with determination and endurance shall be united in one soundly constructed and perfection in body, as for countless years we have aspired to produce him both for breeding purposes and work.'

The lively intelligence and mental alertness of the Dachshund, combined with its refined manners and engaging form, together with its unswerving loyalty, have gained the breed great popularity. It is a great pity that so many owners have lost sight of the fact that the breed was evolved for a purpose. The forester's Dachshund accompanies him all through the day. In the evening the dog is not shut up, rather he is allowed to sleep where he wishes, and to accompany his master to the café.

A goodly part of every Dachshund's life should be spent in the open air, with freedom to dig and hunt.

As a breed they are amazingly accommodating and can adapt themselves to life in a city, with a flat for home. But the pleasure he will get from a walk in the country and the chance to work a rabbit-scented hedge, should convince the owner that the breed is not meant to live in a town.

A fat, soft, flabby Dachshund much resembling a coffee table, is a pathetic sight. A hard conditioned dog can go anywhere and never tires. The fat dog is lethargic and, incapable of leading a normal active life, he tends to become unhappy and stupid. Too many owners think they are being kind to their Dachshund in sharing tit-bits with him, this is the reverse. A dog living a perfectly natural life can be kept in condition and health on a diet of meat, and brown bread baked hard in the oven.

The fat Dachshund cannot do a long walk, as a result of the fatness the feet will probably be soft; this, combined with the heavy weight on the short legs, will cause him soon to tire. If the fat Dachshund is gradually dieted and two walks daily instead of one are started, gradually increasing the length of the distance and the speed at which it is walked, the weight can be reduced.

With the soft feet, the nails will be found to be too long, so preventing the pads from touching the ground evenly. The treatment for long pointed nails is to use a file, gradually working from the side of each nail in turn. This file may be made at home by the purchase of emery paper, Evostik and a piece of wood 9 in long by $\frac{5}{8}$ in by $\frac{3}{8}$ in. Exercise will not cause a Dachshund's feet to become unsound. A correctly made foot is thick-padded and round in shape, with the nails short and the weight of the dog distributed evenly. Exercise will harden the pads, and so make the dog come up on its toes. It cannot thicken flat feet, or correct faulty construction of the anatomy of the forelegs and consequently the feet. Exercise can correct sloppy action and aid somewhat in tighting loose shoulder formation.

Digging is first class exercise for the Dachshund, and the majority will certainly do just this at the slightest opportunity though they may spoil the appearance of the garden, by tunnelling into the herbaceous border. Far too many Dachshunds lead a sedentary existence, this applies particularly to the Miniatures whom one sees walking sedately with their owners in the cities. For perfection these little ones should be allowed freedom to run around, and not exercised only on a lead for a short distance. They may be small, but nevertheless are just as full of energy as their larger relations.

When on a lead a Dachshund must not be allowed to pull. It should be taught to walk on a loose lead on one's left. If this habit has developed, it may be corrected by tapping the dog on the nose with a rolled newspaper every time it lunges forward. Repeat the lesson daily and be firm, but kindly. As stated previously a Dachshund must never be thrashed, for the intelligent dog will become obstinate. A scolding should be indicated by the tone of voice, and the lesson repeated, this gradually curing the bad habit.

Both the long-haired and the wire-haired varieties need no protection against even the coldest weather. Neither appear to notice the cold if correctly fed and housed. Wet weather is not appeciated by the Smooth Hairs, even though they are invariably difficult to keep out of the water for a swim.

11 Breed Standard and Types

General appearance: Long and low, but with compact, well muscled body, bold defiant carriage of head and intelligent expression.

FIGURE 2:
Correct construction of the Dachshund

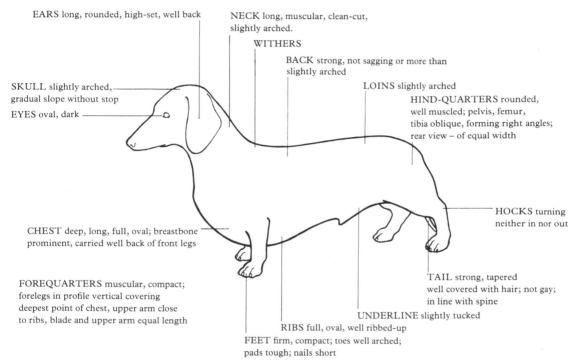

EARS long, rounded, high-set, well back

NECK long, muscular, clean-cut, slightly arched.

WITHERS

BACK strong, not sagging or more than slightly arched

SKULL slightly arched, gradual slope without stop

EYES oval, dark

LOINS slightly arched

HIND-QUARTERS rounded, well muscled; pelvis, femur, tibia oblique, forming right angles; rear view – of equal width

HOCKS turning neither in nor out

CHEST deep, long, full, oval; breastbone prominent, carried well back of front legs

FOREQUARTERS muscular, compact; forelegs in profile vertical covering deepest point of chest, upper arm close to ribs, blade and upper arm equal length

TAIL strong, tapered well covered with hair; not gay; in line with spine

UNDERLINE slightly tucked

RIBS full, oval, well ribbed-up

FEET firm, compact; toes well arched; pads tough; nails short

Characteristics: Intelligent, lively, courageous to the point of rashness, obedient. Especially suited to going to ground because of low build, very strong forequarters, and forelegs, long strong jaw, and immense power of bite and hold. Excellent nose, persevering hunter and tracker.

Temperament: Faithful, versatile and good tempered.

Head and skull: Long, appearing conical when seen from above; from side tapering uniformly to tip of nose. Skull only slightly arched.

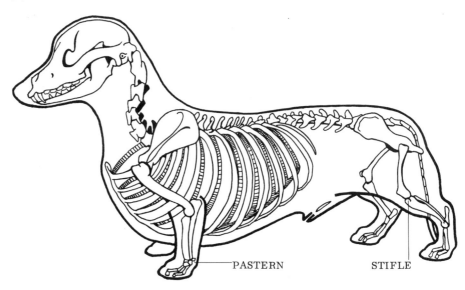

FIGURE 3:
Skeleton of the
Dachshund

PASTERN   STIFLE

Neither too broad nor too narrow, sloping gradually without prominent stop into slightly arched muzzle. Length from tip of nose to eyes equal to length from eyes to occiput. In Wire haired, particularly, ridges over eyes strongly prominent, giving appearance of slightly broader skull. Lips well stretched, neatly covering lower jaw. Strong jaw bones not too square or snipey, but opening wide.

Eyes: Medium size, almond shaped, set obliquely. Dark except in Chocolates, where they can be lighter. In Dapples one or both 'wall' eyes permissible.

Ears: Set high, and not too far forward. Broad, of moderate length, and well rounded (not pointed or folded). Forward edge touching cheek. Mobile, and when at attention back of ear directed forward and outward.

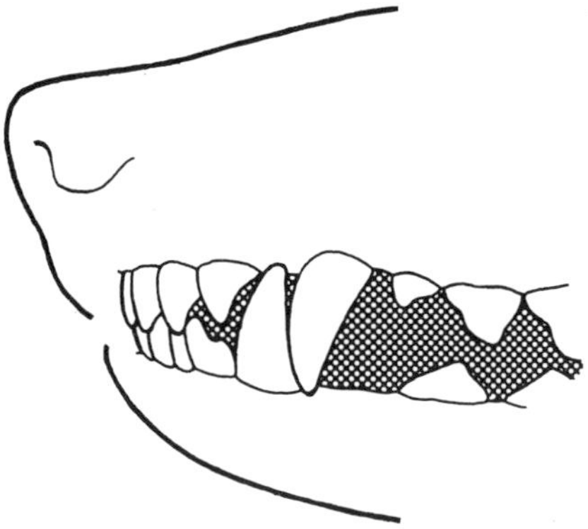

FIGURE 4:
Correct bite. Note
position of canines

Mouth: Teeth strongly developed, powerful canine teeth fitting closely. Jaws strong, with a perfect, regular and complete scissor bite, i.e. the upper teeth closely overlapping the lower teeth and set square to jaws. Complete dentition important.

Neck: Long muscular, clean with no dewlap, slightly arched, running in graceful lines into shoulders, carried proudly forward.

Forequarters: Shoulder blades long, broad, and placed firmly and obliquely (45 degrees to the horizontal) upon very robust rib cage. Upper arm the same length as shoulder blade, set at 90 degrees to it, very stong, and covered with hard, supple muscles. Upper arm lies close to ribs, but able to move freely. Forearm short and strong in bone, inclining slightly inwards; when seen in profile moderately straight, must not bend forward or knuckle over, which indicates unsoundness. Correctly placed foreleg should cover the lowest point of the keel.

FIGURE 5: Forequarters. *Top left*: Correct side view. *Top right*: Correct front view. *Bottom left*: Side view showing fault in rib cage after sixth rib, giving short underline. *Bottom right*: Side view showing leg knuckled over

Body: Long and full muscled. Back level, with sloping shoulders, lying in straightest possible line between withers and slightly arched loin. Loin short and strong. Breast bone strong, and so prominent that a depression appears on either side of it in front. When viewed from front, thorax full and oval; when viewed from side or above, full volumed, so allowing by its ample capacity complete development of heart and lungs. Well ribbed up, underline gradually merging into line of abdomen. Body sufficiently clear of ground to allow free movement.

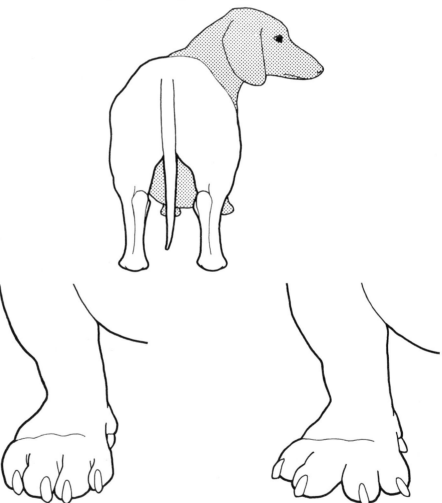

FIGURE 6:
Rear view as it
should
be

FIGURE 7:
Left: Correct foot,
Right: A splayed
foot

Hindquarters: Rump full, broad and strong, pliant muscles. Croup long, full, robustly muscled, only slightly sloping towards tail. Pelvis strong, set obliquely and not too short. Upper thigh set at right angles to pelvis, strong and of good length. Lower thigh short, set at right angles to upper thigh and well muscled. Legs when seen behind, set well apart, straight, and parallel. Hind dew claws undesirable.

Feet: Front feet full, broad, deep, close knit, straight or very slightly turned out. Hind feet smaller and narrower. Toes close together, with a decided arch to each toe, strong regularly placed nails, thick and firm pads. Dog must stand true, i.e. equally on all parts of the foot.

Tail: Continues line of spine, but slightly curved, without kinks or twists, not carried too high, or touching ground when at rest.

Gait/movement: Should be free and flowing. Stride should be long, with the drive coming from the hindquarters when viewed from the side. Viewed from in front or behind, the legs and feet should move parallel to each other with the distance apart being the width of the shoulder and hip joints respectively.

Coat

Smooth-Haired: Dense, short and smooth. Hair on underside of tail coarse in texture. Skin loose and supple, but fitting closely all over without dewlap and little or no wrinkle.

Correct fronts and excellent feet.

Long-Haired: Soft and straight, or only slightly waved; longest under neck, on underparts of body, and behind legs, where it forms abundant feathering, on tail where it forms a flag. Outside of ears well feathered. Coat flat, and not obscuring outline. Too much hair on feet undesirable.

Wire-Haired: With exception of jaw, eyebrows, chin and ears, the whole body should be covered with a short, straight, harsh coat with dense undercoat, beard on the chin, eyebrows bushy, but hair on ears almost smooth. Legs and feet well but neatly furnished with harsh coat.

Colour: All colours allowed but (except in Dapples which should be evenly marked all over) no white permissible, save for a small patch on chest which is permitted but not desirable. Nose and nails black in all colours except Chocolate/tan and Chocolate/dapple, where brown permitted.

Weight & size
   Standards: Ideal weight 20–26 lbs (9–12 kg)
   Miniatures: Ideal weight 10 lbs (4.5 kg). It is of the utmost importance that judges should not award prizes to animals over 11 lbs (5.0 kg)

Faults: Any departure from the foregoing points should be considered a fault and the seriousness with which the fault should be regarded should be in exact proportion to its degree.

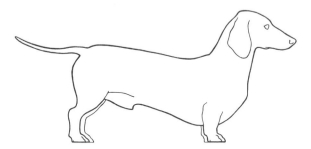

FIGURE 8:
Side view showing rump higher than withers. Compare with figure 2

Note: Male animals should have two apparently normal testicles fully descended into the scrotum.

Type in the Long Hair

A good coated Long Hair needs very little grooming. The hair does not mat, and rain and mud are thrown off instead of penetrating through the hairs. The incorrect coat is one in which the coat stands up, and tends to wave or curl. This type of coat needs much work done on it, for it will become dirty and wet in bad weather. Constant brushing and combing will be needed.

The correct coat should be quite flat and silky with a natural gloss. It should be thick enough on the body to form a protection against wet and cold, but should not obscure the outline of the body. In Germany thick profuse coats are faulted. There and in England the coat on the ears, side of neck, front of chest, underparts, on the back of the forelegs and behind the thighs, should be long and silky – not fluffy. The hair on the tail should be long enough to form a flag, this gradually tapering in length towards the tip of the tail.

Well-set profusely feathered ears are a most attractive feature of this variety. The coat should hang from the tip of the ears and not be confined to the upper parts of the ears only. The hair on the front of the feet, and below the hocks should be short.

A good coated Long Hair needs little show preparation. For exhibition – the feet must be tidied up with scissors; two weeks before the show carefully cut the untidy hair round the foot, neatening the outline – cut away all excess growth of hair between the pads and remove the profuse hair which grows between the toes. This must not be chopped away, but carefully thinned out; if the toe nails are long, either file them, working from the side of each nail, or with nail cutters remove the hooked points to each nail.

If your Dachshund has a flat silky coat, bathing can be undertaken two days before the show. If the coat is coarse and inclined to wave, do this two days earlier. I use Bristow's Lanolin Shampoo.

If your dog has a shortish neck and appears to have a great deal of coat round it, remove some by thinning, either by finger and thumb, or with the back of the comb; the animal's appearance can be improved by adding to the length of neck, which, with an excess of coat, may look stuffy. If for any reason it is not possible to bathe the dog, wash the feathering and the tail flag, and brush the coat thoroughly with one of the coat conditioners, or use Bay Rum. Complete the foot tidying – particularly the outline.

The Long Hair coat is easy to keep in condition with good brushing (with a hard bristled brush) daily; for the feathering behind the legs, the tail and under the chin use a comb.

From time to time discussions can be heard as to the value of coat when assessing a dog in the show ring. An exhibit short of coat, and with the correct silky texture for what it is showing, should be placed above one with a longer, but coarser coat.

The ideal coat is usually slow in growing. Puppies which appear full coated at ten months to a year seldom show the correct silky, flat coat at full maturity. Long Hairs vary very much in the degree to which they lose coats at moulting time. Some lose all the coat, including the feathering, very quickly, others moult so imperceptibly that it is not apparent. In bitches after a litter, the entire coat will be dropped, and many months are needed to complete the new growth. Coat growing can be hastened with a daily brushing, this being done with a bristle brush, and a fine comb; the idea behind this being to stimulate the new growth, and aid in removing the dead hairs.

The coat required by the Standard of Points adds enormously to the appearance of the Long Hair and gives the dog that added appearance of elegance which is so essential to the variety. Too profuse feathering is a fault.

The Long Hair should be similar in all respects to the Smooth Dachshund. It would, however, be a mistake to assume that a first class Smooth could be converted into a first class Long Hair. The short close coat of the Smooth hides nothing of the outline of the body, whereas the coat of the Long Hair, if seen on the Smooth body, would detract in some measure from the length of the Smooth head and the length of back.

Good heavy bone is essential to a Long Hair, this feature is not so pronounced in the Smooths, and when a lightly-boned Long Hair (even with adequate feathering) is seen, the appearance is of weediness and effeminacy. The Long Hair has in large part retained the thick broad foot, which is now seldom seen on the Smooth.

One of the most frequently seen faults in the Long Hair, is the loss of spring of ribbing, tending to make the dog move close in front and behind. The chest must be broad. In this variety length is most important, as is a refined, well proportioned head. *Excessive* depth of chest is undesirable, the same assessment as is applied to the Smooth is called for, i.e. the lowest point of the keel to be level with the wrists. The condition of a too shallow keel is unfortunately to be found in many of the Miniature Long Hairs. Full feathering tends to hide this fault, a competent judge should find this for himself, though from the not too critical onlooker this will be hidden. Loose elbows become apparent when pressure is applied over the withers, though as long as the exhibit stands perfectly still this fault will be concealed.

A long-haired Dachshund should carry its head high on a reachy neck to impart the aristocratic elegance which is, or should be an outstanding characteristic of this lovely variety, whether it be Standard or Miniature.

TYPE IN THE WIRE HAIR

The coat of the Wire-haired Dachshund is unique. It should be distributed and arranged so that at a short distance the dog looks smooth except for the growth of harsh whiskers and the wiry tufts above the eyes. To the touch the hair should be harsh, strong and pliant. When rubbed the wrong way the coat should fall back into place immediately it is left undisturbed. If it does so, the hair forming the top coat will be of the right length and texture. If, on the other hand, the coat stays ruffed up after being stroked against the lie of the hair, it is too long, or too soft, or both. The Standard states plainly that the body coat should be completely even. There should be no appearance of roughness or raggedness. The only parts on which longer hair is required, or permitted, are the jaws and the eyebows. At the sides of the neck, on the front of the chest and at the back of the forelegs the top coat appears to be longer than elsewhere because ridges are formed there by the coming together of hair growing in opposite directions on contiguous parts. The coat must be double. Beneath the wiry coat there should be a close, dense undercoat. This may be seen by raising the top coat, when it will appear as a rather softer, shorter, paler covering, so dense that the skin cannot be seen through it. A double coat of this kind is completely weatherproof and is an efficient protection against thorns. A good coated Wire will go through the thickest undergrowth without hesitation or injury and will finish a day's work in a muddy earth or by a stream side, as clean and dry as when he started.

One sometimes sees a winning exhibit described in a judge's critique as 'a rugged little dog' (meaning untidy). But a dog that looks rugged is not a good Wire. An exhibit that can be justly so described probably has an over-long or open coat and needs tidying up. The coat should lie quite flat on all parts of the body. Even the tufts above the eyes and the small beard should be harsh and, though standing out from the shorter coat on other parts, should not be exaggerated into drooping fringes. The eyebrows and beard are needed to protect the eyes and muzzle as the dog pushes through thorny undergrowth or narrow, rocky tunnels in pursuit of its quarry. To serve that purpose they must be harsh, close and fairly short. The hair on the forelegs is usually rather longer than on the trunk, but, though some latitude may be permitted here, it must not be overdone. Wires which appear to have their forelegs encased in leggings, are nearly always soft in coat. Too much hair on the forelimbs, especially if it is at all soft, is a handicap to a working dog, for it tends to collect mud and may be a serious inconvenience on wet or boggy ground.

The ideal coat needs no trimming, but this perfect covering is, and it must be confessed, always has been, rare. Many Wires with good harsh coats of the right length grow a sort of ruff on the sides of the neck. This should be thinned prior to a show, otherwise the neck will look short and heavy. There may also be a superfluity of hair where the neck runs into the shoulders. This, too, should be thinned to bring out the slight arch at the nape and to make the back line clean and sharp. Bunchy hair above the withers detracts from the appearance of length in both neck and body and may cause the shoulders to look loaded. This is all the trimming a Wire should need and the tidying up should be done a fortnight before the show, to give the coat time to settle.

A FEW HINTS ON TRIMMING FOR NOVICES
(Reprint of article written by the late Mrs M. Howard.)
    'The first thing is to get the right instruments and a comfortable table. There is nothing more uncomfortable than having the dog on too low a table. I had one made, on castors, and it reaches to just about my waist and has a large deep drawer so that everything is to hand.
    'You need a good stripping knife, and I also use a cut-throat razor, which I sharpen on a small stone, and you get a wonderful edge on them but they are a bit awkward in places owing to the long handle, hence the knife (one small one with a blunt end and one saw-edged one), a chalk block, a pair of scissors, some powdered resin and a taper and, lastly, a fine comb.
    'There are three types of coat in the Wire; No. 1, the perfect "pin wire" coat, which only needs tidying; No. 2 the rather full coat with a good undercoat which needs stripping down twice a year, and quite a bit of tidying before shows; No. 3 the real soft coat which to the experienced eye is impossible to trim up and disguise. The hair on the legs, head and ears is always soft. There are a few Smooth judges who do not seem to worry about coats unless the dog is brought into the ring looking like a Dandie!
    'The No. 1 coat, which only needs tidying, requires attention to the tail, feet, legs and head. The finger and thumb (rubbed with powdered resin for a better grip) will remove all the unwanted untidy hairs. The underline will probably also require some attention. I propose going into the trimming of the No. 2 coat in detail, and you can work on the No. 1 coat, in the few necessary places on the same lines.
    'The No. 2 coat is a double coat, the top hair becomes fairly profuse, and there is a close undercoat. (This undercoat is totally lacking in the soft coated specimens). Never try to prepare your dog a week or so before the show. If you are taking the top coat on the back off, do it a month before the show. Trimming of other parts can be left until much nearer the time. Get your kennel dog stripped down no later than October as you cannot remove a warm coat from a dog who lies in kennels in midwinter. A house dog is easier to manage, as he can wear a snug knitted coat when he goes out. He will probably then return from a nice expedition into the brambles with a few strands of wool hanging round his neck which is rather discouraging! It has happened to me before now to come to with a bump a couple of weeks before

Cruft's upon discovering a coat which should have been dealt with in the autumn and has somehow got overlooked. A frenzied effort at reducing some of the longer and thicker hairs has produced a somewhat moth-eaten effect.

'*The Back*: use a razor and take all the top coat right down. Pay particular attention under the tail, around the anus and leave no stray untidy hairs there.

'*Underline*: study your dog as he stands and do away with the hairs that give an untidy underline. Use scissors to neatly trim off all hairs on the end of the sheath. Also with scissors, cut the long hairs inside the flanks.

'*Neck and chest*: trim right down. There is always a ridge of hair just in front of the shoulders, where the chest hair meets the back hair. Get rid of this ridge. Experience only will teach you what hair to leave if your dog is out at elbows. A little 'padding' of hairs helps to fill up the gaps!

'*Head*: finger and thumb is best here. You want a flat, neat and tidy appearance at the head and hair under the eyes must be removed. A knife is too dangerous here. Some dogs have a 'cow-lick' along the nose; this must be left neat and flat. Decide how much beard you are going to leave. A good beard looks very nice. Comb the beard well forward and strip flat from behind that line. If there is any hair hanging below the ear flaps, remove it either with scissors or finger and thumb. Scissors can be used to shorten the long hair that always grows inside the ear flap at the top.

'*Tail*: the tail must be neat and have no untidy hair on it. Use the knife on the underneath of the tail to remove all protruding hairs and if necessary thin out the top of the tail. Do not leave a lot of long ends on the tip of the tail, taper them to a point to just cover the tail tip.

'*Forelegs*: take all the long hair away from the front of the forelegs; if you leave too much there it tends to give a 'knuckled-over' unsound appearance. You want a nice lot of hair at the back of the forelegs. You aim at absolute round well-padded feet, and if your dogs fail in this respect you can help with 'trimming'. Put the foot flat on the table and cut all round into a neat shape with scissors. Then go over the foot with a taper which removes 'the cut' look.

'*Hindlegs and feet*: clean all hair off the hocks. You aim at a neat shapely hindfoot with no 'frills'.

'Lastly, do not forget to put your dog into the ring with ears that are clean and teeth free from tartar.'

An experienced judge can always tell if a coat is in its natural state or whether it is only partially grown following stripping. However expert the trimmer, a trimmed Wire when placed against one with the correct natural coat looks glaring artificial, and the contrast becomes additionally evident when the coat is handled. When judging Wires it is essential to run the hand over and through the coat to assess its length and texture. If an exhibit has been stripped within a week or two of a show, the top coat will not have grown sufficiently for its texture to be felt. I have known bad-coated dogs to be shown in this condition; the owners hoping the judge will regard such exhibits as being 'out of coat' and give them the benefit of the doubt as to what their top coats would be in respect of length and texture when fully grown. Because of the impossibility of forming any reliable opinion on the nature of the top coat until it is fairly well grown, exhibits shown in their 'under-vests' should always be penalised. To assume their coats would be correct if properly grown is grossly unfair to other competitors.

A judge should give credit only for what he can see and assess during the time an exhibit is in the ring. There can be no justification for giving an exhibit that is out of coat full marks because on a previous occasion it has been shown with a perfect coat. In making his awards a judge should be guided by neither prophecy nor memory. On the other hand, it is unfair seriously to fault an exhibit which, though having a harsh, short, double coat, is somewhat short of hair on chin and eyebrows. The ideal coat is slow in growing. Often a Wire destined to have a perfect coat when fully mature will look almost smooth up to a year old, and may be twice that age before it acquires full furnishings. But even while these are growing the texture, length and lie of the body coat and the destiny of the undercoat may be judged, so that, though a few marks may be deducted for lack of eyebrows and beard, the exhibit should score more points for coat than a competitor shown in full coat of indifferent texture.

Novice breeders are sometimes dismayed to find puppies in litters bred from wire-haired parents looking quite smooth coated for some weeks after birth, and wonder what has gone wrong. So far from this being a cause for worry, it is a most encouraging sign, for whelps that show a wiry coat before the age of ten weeks or so are likely to grow into bad-coated adults. Until they are four months old the smoother the pups look the better. After that age close examination will reveal longer hairs beginning to appear on the muzzle, between the toes and on the forelegs. By running the hand along the back against the lie of the hair the coat will be found to be slightly longer and coarser than in Smooth puppies of similar age. Thereafter the coat becomes longer and harsher as the weeks pass, till by the time they are six months old the youngsters will be clearly wire-haired. In the past many novices have bitterly regretted the impatience that prompted them to dispose of their smooth-coated puppies as pets and to retain the long-coated ones for future breeding and showing.

The revival of the Wire-haired Dachshund that has taken place during the past twenty years has been accompanied by a great improvement in type. The length of body, the top line, the length and depth of keel, are vastly more to the desired standard. The faulty running up top line is seldom seen; shoulder placement is inclined to be too forward, and the upper arm too short.

The intercrossing of the Smooth and Wire coat which was prevalent shortly after World War II, (this with intent to increase the length) is no longer permitted by the Kennel Club. In Germany the mating of the Smooth to Wire is now forbidden though some of the Wires still have 'Smooth type head' having lost the original broader muzzle of the Wire owing to the cross. Indiscriminate crossing of Wire and Smooth could be disastrous, producing faults from which the Wire is free, also leading to the appearance of Smooth pups in Wire litters. The Wire coat is dominant to that of the Smooth, if however, there has been, *no matter how far back* in the pedigree, an introduction of the Smooth, this will reappear as a recessive many generations later.

The admirers of the Wire Hair have a thriving Club devoted to the variety and the Trophies owned by the Club are on offer to its members at both Open and Championship shows. There is a Club magazine for all members whether exhibitors or pet owners.

12 The Dapple

The dapple pattern is a very old coloration. First mention of it can be traced back to 1797.

In 1889 there appeared in Germany a few silver grey (silver dapple) Dachshunds. The theory at the time was that they were the result of continuous breeding of chocolates with each other. Previously to this the breeding of black and tan to black and tan through the process of dilution of the colour factor, resulted in the appearance of chocolates. These were followed by the coat colour in some cases turning to chocolate tigers (in England 'dapples'). They were even more lacking in pigment than the silver greys or silver dapples, the coat colour being a bluish grey on a chocolate ground.

The first dapple to be seen in England was Tiger Reinecke, imported in 1890. Other dapples were brought to this country up until the outbreak of the First World War. They were used at stud with some success.

Following the war only one dapple remained – Pied Piper – he, when ten years old, was mated to a black and tan bitch; from this union two puppies were whelped, one being a chocolate and a silver dapple, who became Ch. Foxsilver. He can be found at the back of the pedigrees of the Smooth Standard dapples of the present time.

The breeding of dappled Dachshunds has continued in England and a great improvement in type of this unusual colour has been noticed. Previous to the start of World War II the dapples as a whole were not comparable with the whole colours. Too little thought had been given to breeding the correct type, and too much attention paid to the colour. This resulted in animals that could not compete and win, in the classes allocated to the breed. It became the norm to find at Club Shows special classes for dapples.

The pattern, be it silver, chocolate, or red dapple, is dominant and cannot be found in litters bred from whole coloured parents. One of these must be a dapple, even if only showing a few silver hairs, or maybe a fleck in an eye. This is sufficient to transmit the colour pattern and may very possibly result in some of the litter being well dappled. The mating of dapple to dapple as previously stated, results in a large percentage of albinos. If some of the progeny of such a mating escape this defect, the markings will show large patches of white with red or chocolate body colour and cannot really be called dapple. A true dapple is *not* white, though there will probably be white flecks through the dapple coat pattern.

The colour pattern for a silver dapple should have the whole ground colour of the coat, a bright silver grey, made up of a mixture of black and white hairs in about equal proportion – so giving a roan effect – on this ground irregular shaped patches of black are distributed. For perfection, no part of the body or limbs should show any large unbroken areas of black. In this colouring the roan effect gradually fades with age, the areas of black increasing in size, with reduction of the silver grey.

In chocolate dapples the ground colour consists of a mixture of chocolate and silver-white hairs and the patches are chocolate. The red dapple is like the chocolate, except that the coloured hairs in the ground colour, and the solid patches, are deep red. In silver and red dapples the nose must be black, whilst in the chocolates this is brown. Eyes may be brown or wall, that is blue or whitish. For perfection, the eye should tone in with the hue of the surrounding area. No large patches of white are permissible in a show dapple (except in the U.S.A.).

The dapple pattern can be seen to best advantage in the Wire Hairs, tracing this back to the introduction of the Schnauzers with their silver grey coats. The Wire dapples, usually brindle or chocolate, are more numerous than in the Smooth variety.

The Miniature Wires go from strength to strength following importation of Aggi (Schmidt) – the silver dapple. She can be traced in direct descent from Peter von der Hirschau, a silver dapple whelped in 1910. There is mention of a silver grey Wire, Suschen Waldhaus (five generations behind Aggi) who in turn was sired by a Smooth dapple – Tristram vom Luitpoldspark, the double grandson of Peter von der Hirschau. Aggi's son Huntersbroad Graphite whelped in 1953 was not only a bright silver dapple but a dog of excellent type and much used at stud. His descendants in many kennels have reached a high standard in England. On the Continent, Mme Suzanne de Bernes, now living in France and referred to under the heading of the Miniature Wires, owns, and has shown with great success, amongst others, Rigol Smoking Jacket, a near descendant of Aggi. This dog takes back to the discerning breeders of Germany, France and Italy, a typical English bred Wire with a background pedigree approved by the Teckel Klub.

The Miniature Smooths had not previously had any outstanding specimen of this coat pattern till Mr Negal of the Montreux kennel decided to accept a challenge to breed a champion in this variety. He bought a lightweight silver dapple (carrying the blood of Ch. Zeus as indeed do all the Montreux through Kisska von der Howitt, dam of Ch. Contessina) and mated her to one of his line bred studs for the second generation breeding back to the grandsire. From this mating he bred a dog to become the first Miniature Dapple Champion in England, the chocolate dapple Bellini, who was eventually sold to France.

The German silver dapple Long Hair Alke vom Dangelshübel – pictured below – is a silver dapple bred from a black and tan sire ex a

Rigol Smoking Jacket by Ch. Rigol Willy Dhu ex Rigol Phantom of Frejendor. Owned and bred by Madame Suzanne de Bernes

Alke vom Dangelshübel by Lachs von Geiseltal ex Koralle vom Dangelshübel. Owned and bred by Frau Pautsch.

white and brown dapple dam, who was by the red dapple sire and ex a silver dapple dam, the American bred Dapple Down's Bouquet. The brown dapple and white, Koralle vom Dangelshübel, whose sire the red dapple Tupfel vom Dangelshübel, is also ex the American Dapple Down's Bouquet. The American import, Bouquet, is ex a Smooth chocolate dapple and sired by a Long Hair. The type shown by Alke is very satisfactory and her markings well defined.

Reading an article on dapples in the *American Dachshund*, I realised that those breeders who specialise in the colour (there are many of them with a large number of these patterned dogs), mix both coats and colours, and double up on the dapple breeding. The article warns the breeder to 'avoid dapple-to-dapple breeding which can produce the homozygous dapple (double dapple) unless you are very lucky and very patient, very practical, and highly breeder-oriented.'

The double dapple can *only* produce dapple offspring, regardless of whether bred to a dapple or a solid-colour dog. In a dapple-to-dapple breeding programme you will want some experience as a breeder especially in the area of disappointment, for breeding the double dapple can be heartbreaking. The animal appears with white over the body; where the single dapple may have one blue eye, or an eye with blue flecks slightly visible, the double dapple is very likely to have two blue eyes; one of these may be reduced in size or non-existent.

There may be a minute eye slot with no eye concealed inside, the dog may also be deaf. Continuing from Mrs Crary's article and her recent letter, 'out of five double dapple matings whelped in the kennel, only two have been deaf, all blue-eyed, and one with a tiny eye opening containing no eye-ball, this one is also deaf. This one at birth had both eyes located in darkly pigmented areas, and we hoped she would have dark eyes. Of other homozygous dapples whelped in this kennel the number of deaf ones is very low, and only about 50 per cent of them have functional eyes of reduced size.' The little bitch with no eyes and no hearing surprisingly was allowed to grow on and 'she is incidentally, a well adjusted pet with a terrific nose and the ability to detect movement of her family from vibrations on the floor in her house.'

Mrs Crary used a Long Hair double dapple of her breeding as mate for a Blue smooth-haired bitch. The sire was deaf. One of the resulting litter is a finished Champion, a second has one major win and a number of lesser points towards its championship. This one Mrs Crary has used for what she describes as her finest bitch, Ch. Sangsavant Justine, herself the daughter of an English born bitch (Rockfall Maid Marion). Colour is not mentioned, Mrs Alison Hay (Rockfall) to my knowledge did not have dapples; 'three fine animals have started on a show career'.

I wonder just what Madame Rikovsky and our Angel Negal would have to say about such intensive inbreeding. It did not aid their dapple production!

Long Hair Dachshunds were the last of the three coats in England to include the dapple pattern, and it came about accidentally. The mating of Wire to Long had been frowned upon for years, and then, in 1977, the K.C. forbade the crossing of coats and sizes. However the dapple had appeared in the Miniature Longs through an accidental mating of mother to son – Mrs Wharton's Littlenodes Mother of Pearl and Littlenodes Quicksilver. They produced four pups, one black and tan, one silver dapple (perfectly marked), one blue merle and one white. Littlenodes White Knight is one of the rarities, being neither blind nor deaf.

The silver dapple dog became Ch. Littlenodes Silver Smoke in the ownership of Mrs Owen, and has Champion children to his credit. Littlenodes Quicksilver went to the owner of his sire, Mrs Palmer, and had one certificate to his credit.

A genetic defect has appeared in the Miniature Longs carrying the

Gingerblue Rose of Sharron with nine dapple puppies sired by a double dapple (homozygous). Owned by Sharron and Jerry Cox of Houston, Texas.

dapple blood, that of umbilical hernias. Wires are frequently born with this congenital trouble (though this is easily corrected by the vet).

I remarked earlier in the chapter on the dapple pattern of the coats of the Wires who carry this colour, and traced the ancestry of the wire coat back to the Schnauzer. I have followed this up and under the microscope the examination of both the plain and coloured hairs from a long-hair coat, shows the variance in coat structure; that of the dapple-hair showing bands cross-wise in each hair (Schnauzer legacy), the plain hairs giving no picture of cross banding.

The Dapple Dachshund *Some thoughts on breeding and terminology* *by Suzanne de Bernes*

It's as difficult to write clearly and concisely about dapple breeding as it is to breed a Champion dapple Dachshund. This is because of the enormous confusion which has grown up in connection with the description of colours and the dapple pattern.

Everyone knows how easily word meanings and names can become distorted. But Latin words and names have been in use for hundreds of years to enable interested people of the world to discuss and identify flora and fauna without risk of confusion.

Similarly, there is a correct genetical terminology – proof against misunderstanding – to describe colours and markings in the animal world. There are many reference books available for interested dog breeders and a great deal of work and research has been done to help them.

The dominant merle factor is inherited in a few breeds of dogs, including the Dachshund, or Teckel (to give him a popular name). In the universal language of genetics, this factor is known as M. It can take two forms: Mm denotes *Homozygous*, MM denotes *Heterozygous*.

This merle factor affects the pigmentation of skin and coat hairs: it therefore produces characteristic patterns on the coats of dogs which inherit it, and in most breeds its presence is denoted by the word *merle*. So, just as there are merle Collies, merle Cardigan Corgis and so forth, there are also merle Teckels. But unfortunately for breeders of Teckels who have become interested in the merle factor, other names for this distinctive appearance of the coat have been thought up to confuse the picture.

Merle Teckels in England and America are known as Dapples; in France and Italy they are Arlequin and Arlecchino respectively, and in Germany, Tiger. The last name suggests a striped Teckel, and in fact there are a very few striped Teckels; but these are brindles, with the genetical terminology *eb*.

What can be done to unify the enthusiasts of a three-colour job?

Another question is whether merle, or dapple, is a colour or a pattern.

The answer lies in the effect of the merle factor on the skin and coat; it reduces the pigmentation in some areas and leaves other patches with darker hairs. For example, the action of a merle gene on a black and tan dog is to reduce the black pigmentation, producing silver patches: in chocolate and tan it produces beige patches. Then there is the problem of how to describe the colour and pattern so that the description is universally understood. But first, one must have a clear idea of the difference between colour and pattern. The merle blotches or patches, being lighter in colour, may logically be regarded as the pattern; thus one could simply use the 'general colour' word first, and the 'pattern' word second. Here are some examples, arranged in order of colour dominance, of how this naming system would work: Brindle dapple, red dapple, black dapple, chocolate dapple.

In Germany, this is the method actually used. They say Saufarbentiger, Rottiger, Schwarzetiger, Brauntiger; 'Tiger' being the word for dapple as we have already mentioned.

The use of the word 'brindle' is also very confusing. Brindle is an admixture of different coloured hairs in Teckels, and is found in reds, black and tans, and chocolates. But its literal meaning is 'branded' or 'striped' and brindle does appear as a striped pattern on some breeds, including certain strains of Teckels, as we have already noted. Therefore, from breed to breed, brindle has acquired two meanings. Are we talking about hair mixture, or are we talking about stripes? In the genetic terminology, confusion vanishes, because there are two separate genetic symbols for both meanings. 'Striped' *eb* 'Overall' (basic mixture) *ay*.

Brindle becomes 'wild boar' and 'pepper and salt' in Europe, but I will continue to use the word brindle because that is the word used in the U.S.A. and in England.

This genetic factor increases the usual number of Teckel colours by one for each colour, in the following way: Red, red brindle; black and tan, black and tan brindle; chocolate, chocolate brindle. Consequently, it also affects the dapples as any one of these brindles can be mated to a dapple, so we have: Brindle dapple (black and tan brindle with lighter brindle pattern); red brindle dapple (red brindle with lighter brindle pattern); chocolate brindle dapple (chocolate brindle with lighter chocolate brindle pattern).

In my experience of breeding these colours and patterns, I have seen clearly the differences between brindle dapple and basic dapple puppies at a very early age. Brindle hairs can be seen within hours of the puppy's birth, whereas black dapples appear to be virtually black and white at that very early stage.

My endeavour has been to breed black dapples and chocolate dapples, rather than brindle or red dapples. As brindle and red are first and second in order of dominance, I have tried to eliminate them and bring out the recessive by constant introduction of black and tan. With this object I have bred all my dapples to my black and tans, and occasionally to my chocolate and tans; using this method I have not had a red dapple since 1956.

In the litters produced according to this plan, I nearly always get an assortment of different coloured progeny, with the occasional appearance of a brindle or a brindle dapple. As one should always keep the best of the litter for future breeding, one must count oneself extremely fortunate to have bred a topnotch dapple – irrespective of its colour – because quality must come first. Therefore, I thought I was very lucky in this lottery to have bred two important stud dogs at an early stage. In 1959 came Rigol Phantom Phillip, a black dapple, whom I mated to my black and tan and chocolate and tan females. The other was Champion Rigol Willy Dhu, a black and tan, in 1960, who was mated to my brindle, black and chocolate dapple females. Both the original Wire imports carried chocolate, so throughout this breeding period chocolate and tans, and chocolate dapples appeared. Any brindle dapples, male or female, were bred to black and tans, as previously mentioned.

In order to exclude brindles, I have never used them for breeding, but the brindle dapples I continue to breed to black and tan, resulting in a majority of black dapple progeny. This may be due to consistent use of black and tan in my breeding programme in the endeavour to cast out the dominant brindle colour.

Over many years of dapple breeding, I have only bred for heterozygous dapples. On average I have had a 50–75 per cent Mm progeny in each litter, the remainder of the litter being black and tan or chocolate and tan with the occasional brindle and tan. In only one of my litters was there no dapple progeny, maybe due to the fact that that particular litter was numerically small – only two puppies.

In all except three matings, I have mated heterozygous dapples Mm to other coloured Teckels but in the main have used black and tan with chocolate, as recessive. The exceptional three matings referred to above were the matings of two dapples Mm together. Here are the results:

Litter No. 1	3 dapples MM
Litter No. 2	2 black dapples Mm
	2 black and tans
Litter No. 3	1 brindle, 1 brindle dapple Mm
	1 chocolate dapple Mm
	1 white dapple MM

Two interesting points emerge from these matings: first, there was only one white dapple among the eleven offspring. Second, the Mm puppies in these three litters were neither brighter in colour nor clearer – nor more profuse – in pattern than the Mm dapples from my usual mating with one Mm parent.

As most breeders know, there is a great loss of pigmentation in mating reds to chocolates and tans; the red progeny can have chocolate noses and light coloured nails. It is not true that the merle factor in its single form (Mm) weakens pigmentation in these areas, and one can nearly always trace such weakening to red chocolate matings. For this reason, I have always refused to allow any chocolate male to mate with red females, and the same applies with chocolate dapple to red, or red dapple to chocolate.

I have always kept very complete records of all progeny bred by me, and bred from females mated to my dogs, and my experience over a very long period of years has led me to the conviction that there is very little possibility of forecasting with any degree of certainty the colours of a future litter from dapple Mm to other colours.

Direction away from colours that you wish to avoid and a steady course towards the desired colours, plus a thorough knowledge of the ingredients of your own stock, is the best policy for the achievement of your objective.

One black dapple I bred had no more silver hairs on her than could be covered by a small coffee spoon – the rest was all black and tan. She was mated to a black and tan dog, and she produced five puppies: one black and tan, and *four* veritable leopards! I mention this as an example of how careful one must be to recognise a dapple. The smallest dapple mark cannot be overlooked, because, owing to the dominance of the dapple gene, it is bound to emerge in the progeny when the dog is mated, and often emerges in dramatic form. Mistakes and 'surprises' when puppies are born may well be the result of failure to detect a minute dapple trace on one of the parents.

It is also very important to register all dapple pups as dapple. In the lighter coloured dapples – the red dapples and light brindle dapples – the even paler markings can 'fade out' at an early age, so that to all intents and purposes these youngsters appear to be a light brindle or red from then onwards, and for the rest of their lives. But breeding from these subjects will always prove their dapple inheritance.

Conversely, no Teckel without a trace of dapple pattern will ever produce dapples unless it is mated to a dapple, even though one or both of its parents may have been a dapple (Mm).

In black dapples, even the tiniest mark of silver, in my experience, never fades, and it can be clearly seen throughout the dog's life. This brings us to the thousand-dollar question. At what point – and from what origin – did the merle gene enter as a dominant factor into the genetical make-up of the Teckel? I'm still working on this one! I had an amusing and interesting experience recently worth mentioning in this context. I was showing two Miniature Wire black dapples, both females, to an Austrian judge. One of these dogs was very evenly marked, the other had very few and small markings. The judge told me that one was a 'real Tiger' and the other was 'Gefleckt'. (Two different genetic factors.) Gefleckt! Here is another word to add to the glossary of confusing terminology.

'Our dapples' are a real test for the judge. They are one of the earliest colours in Teckels and it is said that these colours were more visible when hunting, especially on forest land. They certainly are distinguished! But for the breeder and judge they pose a problem, because the dapple pattern can destroy a virtue or enhance a fault simply by optical illusion! I have bred a dog who carries the dark hair vertically from neck to lower arm, giving him in profile a 'straight shoulder' look. On the other hand, if the dark pigmented hair were placed in the correct equal lengths at a 90° angle, it could effectively camouflage unequal length of shoulder to upper arm and oblique angulation. Backlines can appear to dip here and there. But one of the most deceptive sights of all is a dog advancing towards you with one half of his front black and the other half silver!

Considering this, one must be extra careful when manually examining a dapple on the table, one just cannot trust one's eyes for these details when a dog is 'on the move'.

Moreover, judges' reports are not only written for the owners of winning dogs. There are times when a breeder cannot attend shows for some months, and may be eagerly scanning the judges' reports for a future stud. I have had a personal experience of this situation. I showed a brindle male in England who was reported erroneously at two consecutive Championship Shows as being a dapple. This was a double disservice to me, and the absent breeder seeking a stud, because that breeder might not wish to breed dapples, and would in consequence 'strike out' my winning dog from a short list of possibilities. Furthermore, that same breeder (maybe not mentioning that a litter with dapples was required) might send the female to this 'reported' dapple male, and be extremely surprised and disappointed to find no dapple puppies in the subsequent litter! One can only blame the inaccuracy of the judge's report.

What does all this add up to?

To succeed as a dapple breeder you need to produce top show quality, and the correct colour and sex to fit your breeding programme. Your ambition is to breed at least one or two puppies in each litter which carry all these attributes. But nature is hardly ever on your side. And that is why I think that the breeding of show dapples presents to the Teckel breeder the greatest challenge of all.

13 The Versatile Dachshund

The small dog is not only a devoted addition to the household in which he lives, but if given the chance, can excel in the exercise of his inheritance, for a hunting dog is he. Quoting from an article in *The Shooting Times and Country Magazine* – 'Suki, a black and tan miniature Wire, was purchased as first pick of a litter of five whose impeccable antecedents included a German born paternal grandfather, while several ancestors had amply proved their worth as woodland stalking companions'. Her dam had been entered to deer by the breeder, a Forestry Commission stalker, shooting one, dragging its carcass a hundred yards or so through the undergrowth and putting the already eager bitch on to its line. The dog led her owner straight to the deer.

Suki was introduced to elementary field training at $5\frac{1}{2}$ months. 'I had to decide whether to leave her in the car or whether to let her walk with me and take my chance on her youthful exuberance putting a possible quarry to flight and thereby spoiling my chance of a shot. I stopped in mid-stride when I saw a roebuck walking across my front on the pasture, about 70 yards away. Having assessed the buck and decided that it was cullable, I executed a quick flanking movement with a view to intercepting it when it crossed the ride.

'The little dog sat quite still while I took up a kneeling position. When I fired the deer plunged forward, throwing its hindlegs high in the air, then ran awkwardly for a few yards along the ride before turning into the plantation. The puppy having stayed obediently still for the prescribed waiting period, moved forward with me mildly interested in the scent from the blood spots, and realised that she was expected to find something. When we came up to the fallen deer, she merely stepped over its legs and carried on sniffing with her back to the carcass.

'It was a different matter entirely when I offered the puppy a titbit from the emergent bullet-hole. She protested when I tethered her while I dragged the roebuck's carcass well out of sight and when I went back for her she led me straight to the deer. I repeated this manoeuvre, this time zig-zagging through cover, as I towed the carcass, so as to make the puppy's task more difficult. Again she followed up eagerly, although briefly at fault at one point, she quickly cast back and recovered the line.'

Further to the earlier reference to Colonel Phipps and his Talavera Dachshunds and quoting from a letter by him: 'Linda is a three year old bitch, a granddaughter of Ch. Zeus vom Schwarenberg, were it not for one rather crooked foreleg, she would be a very high class show bitch. She excels very much in length and strength of foreface and has a lovely shoulder. These two points to my mind are the most important of all in a dog required for underground work. The foreface because it gives them strength in jaw and keeps the enemy away from their eyes in an underground battle. The shoulder because it enables them to get in and still more important get out of a small or narrow hole without getting wedged in by a root or projecting rock or stone.

'I wish that you could have had the view of Linda that I had last week from the top of my horse. She had a fight with and then bolted a hard run fox from a drain well over 40 yards long. I saw her emerge just behind the fox, snapping at its brush and then with ears flapping in the most fascinating way pursue the fox across a large field until overtaken by the hounds to whom she so obviously "handed over" for the job to be finished off. It was one of the most breath-taking animal sights I have ever seen.'

Then to quote from a shooting man, 'I can confirm the abilities of the Dachshund as a working dog and was pleasantly surprised when I first discovered what a good nose my little bitch possessed. This I first realised when taking a walk over the Wiltshire Downs. Included in the company was my Labrador dog (over whom I shot regularly) and a Cocker Spaniel who was also trained to the gun, my Dachshund bitch and a friend. During the walk I marked the run of a hare which crossed our line some distance away. All three dogs crossed the run of the hare, but it was only the little Dachshund bitch who picked up the scent and she was most noisy in acclaiming the fact and followed the run of the hare for some distance until called off. As an additional check we walked some distance away from the run and about ten minutes later again crossed the run. Again the two other dogs crossed without picking up the scent, but this was not the case with the little Dachsie who was allowed to follow the scent and finally nose the hare. This performance was indeed amazing to me, in particular that the Dachshund had, up to then, not been shot over. I have since shot over her on many occasions and always found her nose to be a particularly keen one and as well able as other gun dogs to discriminate between the scent of a pheasant, partridge, hare or rabbit. I got to know her so well that finally I could judge reasonably accurately the type of game she had winded, the basis being mainly the degree of excitement she displayed. My main objection to her was her noisiness which almost equalled a Cocker Spaniel. But as I have mainly shot over a Labrador, perhaps I am rather critical in this respect.'

History was made in England in 1970, for in that year the first Dachshund, a red Long-haired bitch, Siebe Konigen von Mayrhofen, owned by Captain and Mrs Thompson stationed with the U.S. forces in this country, won the Obedience Challenge Certificate in the run off with a big winning Obedience Champion Border Collie bitch. Siebe later gave a demonstration of her superlative work at the Open Show run annually by the Long-haired Club. The impression she gave was of happiness in her responses to commands, she was very evidently out to please her owner/handler.

In the mid-fifties a Miniature Smooth bitch – So Exquisite of Tatnam – T.D., U.D.Ex., C.D., owned and worked by Mrs Ogle at seven Championship Trials, qualified U.D.v.G. and Ex. at each of these events. This bitch being bred from – So Magical of Tatnam – U.D., Ex., C.D.

There are at the present time several Dachshunds to be seen competing in Obedience classes at shows, the majority enjoying their work, and scoring well. It is most noticeable that the Dachshunds take these exercises in good part and show no evidence of boredom.

14 Care of the Dachshund

In the majority of homes the Dachshund is a house pet, and as such probably sleeps in the kitchen. The Smooth varieties are particularly attracted to heat – and quite noticeably expect to be tucked up in a blanket for the night. The Wire and Long Hairs are content to sleep in a box or basket on a rug.

When a puppy joins a new household the owner should from the start assert himself and his authority over the pup. A dog respects the master or mistress who does just this. Dachshunds may be stubborn, but their affection is given to those whom they have to obey.

For the puppy's first night, make sure, before going to bed, that the puppy is not hungry and knows where to find his bed. For the first few nights the addition of a hot water bottle will give the pup the consolation of feeling that its litter mates and their consequent warmth are still around. The new pup probably cries from sheer loneliness. The owner may have to come downstairs during the night and reassure the youngster, but should not relent and carry the pup upstairs – unless that is where one is prepared to let it sleep during its lifetime.

The breeder should have given the new owner a diet sheet; this must be followed carefully. Any sudden change in diet may induce diarrhoea and this can be very stubborn to cure.

It is always more satisfactory for the new pup if there is another dog already installed in the family. No matter how much love and affection the human family will give, there is undoubtedy a great bond between members of the canine world.

As the puppy grows its great intelligence and inordinate curiosity can only develop in an atmosphere of freedom and in close contact with its owner. Undue restraint makes a Dachshund stupid and nervous, and inevitably leads to grossness.

If there are several Dachshunds kept, they will do better if allowed to sleep out of the house. Substantial out-houses or brick-built stables can be adapted for this. A good sleeping box can be made from a tea chest, slightly raised from the ground to avoid a concentration of moisture from the sleeping body. A three inch board should be nailed across the front of the chest to retain the bedding, which should be wood wool, or even better shredded paper from the paper mills. Heat is not necessary, for in a tea chest the reflected heat from the animals in it, provides this. In extreme weather a piece of clean sacking, or an extra board nailed on, reduces the size of the opening. The chest can be scrubbed frequently, and the brick walls of the building kept clean by whitewash. If the owner uses corridor kennels, these should be creosoted. Additional warmth can be provided by lining the walls and roof and packing the interspaces.

Remembering that Dachshunds will dig, and that they may not be welcome in the garden all day, the preparation of an enclosed run with the wire sunk into the ground to a depth of eight inches, will give them a chance to run around and dig. The run could be into an orchard, with adequate space to run about. An unused tennis court is ideal for this purpose. I have seen a large greenhouse with the staging removed, and concrete laid, used as a covered run. This is ideal for the bad weather.

Coats should be attended to daily. A Smooth needs only a rub down with a hound glove; for the Long and the Wire use a stiff bristled brush and a comb. The dogs look forward to this attention and it gives one the chance to make sure that the ears are not needing cleaning, also teeth. Too many Dachshunds do not have suffcient care given to teeth. In many this causes no difficulty, but in some a pale yellow deposit of tartar can be seen over the teeth, and if allowed to remain it gradually forms a hard deposit which then has to be removed under anaesthetic by a vet. To clean teeth, I use the milled edge of a small coin, and still keep a sixpence for this purpose.

By nature a Dachshund is greedy, the adult's diet should, therefore be in the proportion of $\frac{3}{4}$ ounce to each pound of body weight. Meat or fish must provide the major part of this ration; in these days there are several products on the market supplying this need. For fish – rock salmon or coley are readily eaten. Eggs can be used as a supplement and are much enjoyed. The carbohydrate side of the diet can take the form of brown bread which has been rusked in a cool oven. A great treat is to fry a slice of bread before feeding. Cheese can be grated over the main meal, so adding to the necessary protein. Potatoes in any form, and pork products, should not be fed to dogs. Salt is not required. Vitamins as outlined in the puppy rearing chart should be continued through the adult life. During the sunless days, cod liver oil must be added to this diet. The importance of not giving tit-bits must be emphasised, for this is the way to put on that unwanted fat. If the dog tends to be eating well, though remaining thin, instead of using rusked bread, cut the bread into diced portions and pour over the stock or soup. It may be necessary to increase the ration till the weight becomes apparent.

In the unusual event of your Dachshund refusing food though in good health, do not increase the number of meals, but rather offer the dish of food, and if not eaten readily remove it and make the dog wait till the next feeding time. An iron tonic could be given, or the number of vitamin pills increased.

When a Dachshund comes in from exercise wet and muddy, it can rapidly be cleaned and dried by the use of a chamois leather wrung out in warm water. This not only cleans the coat but the drying process is speedy.

15 Exhibiting

For the novice owner and the raw pup, the first attempt at competition should be in a small local show. The various types of shows under the aegis of the Kennel Club, begin with a Sanction event. These have probably only twenty or so classes and one judge for all varieties shown on that day. The next is a Limited show. This type is reserved for members of the particular society for the area. Membership is welcome, and invariably there may be classes for Dachshunds, not many, but sufficient for the newcomer. The youngster can be entered in the lowest class (the definition of all classes scheduled at any show is stated fully in the schedule), this will probably be A.V. (this meaning Any Variety) Dachshund Novice. The judge is frequently one familiar with the breed, so your pup will have the gentle handling so necessary for his first time out. If you are ambitious to try this puppy still further, enter him in the A.V. Puppy Class, so that he can mix with both large and small dogs of a multitude of varieties.

Having tried the pup at a small type show, advance to an Open event. These have several more classes allocated to the breed, and maybe there will be classes for your particular variety of Dachshund. There are, however, several Dachshund clubs who run their own Open shows once a year. These are excellent for the new pup, the classes for the varieties are well thought out and provide opportunities for various age groups, with additional classes for the more advanced winners. It is a mistake to enter a youngster in too high a class, for he will surely be out of his depth amongst the older, and more seasoned exhibits.

The most advanced shows are those known as Championship Shows. It is at these that a dog or bitch wins the necessary awards to complete a Championship. No pup should make its début to the show world in this standard of competition. The day will be long for both him and the owner, the dog will have to be relegated to a 'bench' for hours, and may well be overawed by the barking of nearby dogs; the owner may know no one and consequently feel frustrated, and this nervousness can transmit itself to the dog. Only when both the owner and the dog have had a thorough grounding in the smaller types of shows and the former become acquainted with various exhibitors, is it wise to venture so high.

When handling a dog in the ring do not worry him unnecessarily. The steward will give you your dog's number, this you must wear in a conspicuous position and take your place amongst the other exhibitors. When your turn comes to take the dog up to the judge move unhurriedly to the table, and place your dog as you have taught him to stand, easily. It is probably a good thing to keep a hand on the dog's foreface for by doing this he will be in contact with you and so not lose confidence.

When he has been examined return to your position, and keep your eye on the judge, for when comparing the dogs the judge will look round at the exhibits, and if yours should be sitting down or in a bad position for assessment, this will make the task harder, and the extrovert showman may go over yours.

When you are in the ring, concentrate on your dog. Do not allow him to get under the feet of other exhibitors, or to interfere with the other dogs. It is very annoying to have a dog bark, or generally annoy others, particularly whilst moving round. Do not chat with the other exhibitors, for you may well not see the judge looking towards your dog, and you could be caught with him in a most unfavourable position. It is not etiquette to converse with the judge while judging is in progress, neither is it correct to inform the judge of the dog's name. If you wish to speak with the judge about your exhibit, wait till the judging is finished.

If the exhibitor is a lady, please do not go into the ring carrying a handbag. Both hands will be necesary to get the best out of your dog; and please do dress for the occasion. Ultra short, tight skirts are not the garments for showing Dachshunds. There is quite a lot of forward bending needed and these dogs are near the ground!

There has been much talk recently about the breed being a 'closed shop' in the show ring. Now this is nonsense. 'It's a closed shop' is said about most breeds at one time or another. Sometimes there may be a degree of truth in the statement, but in the main it is an entirely unfair comment. All breeds are dominated to some extent by the top breeder/exhibitors who win consistently by virtue of the number and excellence of the dogs they put in to the show ring.

When a sucessful breeding programme regularly produces numbers of top quality dogs it is only natural that they are going to be more often in the cards than out of them, so by virtue of regular success in the show ring a good breeder/exhibitor will tend to dominate the breed to some extent. What should not be forgotten are the years of hard work put in to achieve this success, years of careful breeding and much campaigning. Having reaching the pinnacle, it is only natural that one will remain there for as long as one continues to bring out first rate stock.

The novice in every breed has all this to combat in the climb to the top. To be honest, isn't that what we all hope to be – tops in our breed?

Don't worry too much about 'closed shop' talk; just breed carefully and campaign hard. If you have got the dogs and the determination you will get to the top. It's the most wonderful sport in the world, so be sporting about it. Enjoy your dogs and enjoy showing them. Just think, when you do reach the dizzy heights of success, of all the pleasure you will get from listening to everyone else moaning the winning YOU do!

In the Dachshund world we have exhibitors who have risen rapidly to Championship honours. First to mind is Mrs Jan Duncombe (now Parden). In 1973 she, as a complete Novice, came into the ring with a very handsome dog bred by herself. The parents were of distinguished breeding, but carrying names the show world was not familiar with. The dog – Ch. Dunbrook Cuddl-e-Dudley – became Champion within ten weeks.

Mr and Mrs Robinson (of the now well-known Jamaneans) started with a good bitch, chose their own sire for her, and made up her daughter. Following this up, they purchased a good daughter of a Champion bitch and crowned her.

Under the Smooth chapter I have mentioned Marilyn and Mrs Norton, with their now well established line.

Then, at Cruft's in 1979, the Wire Hair bitch ticket went to Terony Oakleigh, a very well bred bitch purchased as a foundation by Miss Trim. She had not found Oakleigh easy to show, and had painstakingly started at small shows gradually getting her familiar with noise and handling. This endurance finally won her B.O.B. at the Southern

Ch. Terony Oakleigh by Ch. Daxglade Dancing Major of Swansford ex Silvae Mineasping. Owned by Miss Trim. Bred by Mrs Brown.

Dachshund Championship Show in 1978; in this same year she went on to win the bitch Certificate at Cruft's.

JUDGING

If you think that you are ready to judge, ask yourself these questions:

1 Do I know the Breed Standard?

Do I understand what is meant by the *Standard*?

Do I know why this standard is written in the manner it is and how it was evolved?

2 Do I have some (at least a little) general knowledge about the anatomical structure of our breed – the bones, muscles and ligaments with the tendons?

3 Have I seen and examined a lot of *good* dogs of the varieties, not just my own, but many others?

Have I owned any good dogs of my particular variety?

Have I bred any good dogs of my variety?

4 Have I learned to appreciate a virtue over a fault?

Have I learned to appreciate how very time-consuming and very difficult it is to breed a good Dachshund?

Have I learned that all dogs have faults but that *faults are secondary to virtues*? Have I learned to appreciate the good points in the breed and to forgive the faults in favour of the virtues?

If so, judge if asked. Your entry may be large, just because your opinon will be untested till you have completed your assignment. Judging can be difficult, particularly when the exhibits are mediocre and this is where the novice judge's knowledge will be proved.

Remember that the essential qualities of a good Dachshund are:

Soundness: the interpretation in the Oxford Dictionary is given as: healthy, not diseased nor injured. In the dog world this would read – look for correct construction, with no exaggeration of any part of the skeletal framework, the muscular development must be firm and hard and movement must show the propulsion of the body with purposeful movements of the legs, the whole being the result of correct tension of the muscles, which by their attachment to the bony structure at the correct angles, give a free easy swing to the trunk.

Substance: look for a well rounded body, and not one padded with fat; the muscles should be firm and the animal in hard condition.

Symmetry: this is interpreted as showing the right proportions between the parts of the body, the whole being balanced and in harmony.

'No breeder or judge is really matured until he can properly appraise the fundamentals, and judge the animal as a whole.' This was written in *Our Dogs* in January 1945, and is credited to the famous authority on Boxers, J. P. Wagner of the U.S.A.

16 Diseases and Ailments

The best investment against illness is, of course, correct rearing from early infancy. Adequate feeding and ample exercise, together with the immunisation against the virus diseases of the dog, should stand the Dachshund in good stead throughout his life.

If the puppy has been hand-reared through the loss of his dam, he will not have had the essential antibiotic, direct from the dam, which is to be found in the first flow of milk. This substance, colostrum, protects the puppy for the first few weeks of life, hence the theory that the correct time in the young life for inoculation is around nine weeks.

Modern veterinary medicine appears to have almost mastered the virus of hard pad and of distemper. There are the odd cases in which an animal, even though inoculated, falls victim to one or other of these diseases. It is, however, rare. The liver can be attacked by the virus of hepatitis or Rubarth's Disease, but the puppy if correctly inoculated will have received protection against this by the one combined injection.

Abscesses: Dachshunds tend to develop these quite unexpectedly. The swelling will enlarge quickly, often to the size of a tennis ball. The most frequent area to find an abscess is below the jaw. As the swelling hardens, hot fomentations frequently applied will induce this to burst; when this has occurred, gentle pressure used at the lowest part of the abscess will aid the pus to drain away. The open wound may be dabbed with T.C.P. or similar mild antiseptic applied on a wad of clean cotton wool.

Adder bites: there is frequently a risk of this happening during a dry summer. Speedy action must be taken to prevent the poison entering the circulation and thence to the heart. If this bite is in an extremity, apply a tourniquet between this and the heart to stop the circulation upwards. Then make an effort to destroy the poison locally by causing bleeding. Do this by washing the wound with a strong solution of PERMANGANATE OF POTASH. If by mischance this accident happens away from home out at exercise, every effort must be made to return quickly. In some years when the adder population is high, it would be wise to have in the medicine cupboard, ANTI-VENOM serum from Allen and Hanburys. It is unwise to attempt to suck out the poison, unless great care is taken.

Appetite, lack of: this is usually the sign of worm-infested puppies, although it is also a danger signal symptom of the serious virus infections. In ordinary circumstances the appetite will improve after worming and a change of diet. Take the dog's temperature – normal 101.4 – by inserting the thermometer into the rectum, and if necessary call the vet.

Bad breath: this is commonly caused by an excess of tartar on the teeth. The teeth should be watched carefully from puppyhood and any deposit removed gently by rubbing with a damp piece of cotton wool. If this is not efficient, scrape the tooth from the gum downwards with the milled edge of a small coin – repeating the process daily until the tooth is clean. If a dog has a tendency to an excess of tartar, give a daily dose of Macleans Stomach Powder (1 teaspoonful) reducing the dose to once weekly.

Coccidiosis: this is highly infectious and requires strict hygiene as it is contracted from stools, in which the spore forms of the parasite exist. This parasite is similar to that found amongst poultry and the affected dog will lose weight rapidly. Blood-spattered Diarrhoea is a typical symptom. The veterinary surgeon will give the necessary treatment. The dog must come off raw meat, and the diet consists of milky foods.

Constipation: this is frequently caused by too much starchy food, in excess of raw meat; also by chewing bones instead of gnawing them. Liquid Paraffin or Milk of Magnesia should correct this condition.

Dogs rubbing their rears along the ground: this may be caused by the anal glands, situated on either side of the anus, becoming filled with a foul fluid. When a dog is frightened, this fluid is excreted by reflex action. All animals in the canine world should have these glands emptied regularly, failure to do so may result in an abscess formation. To empty the glands, stand the dog on a table, take in the hand a large piece of cotton wool, lift the dog's tail and press the wad hard against the anus, squeezing the sides of the anus between the fingers.

Ears scratching and flapping: this may be just dirty ears or could be ear mites. These are not visible to the eye and can only be seen under a microscope. If the ears are dirty, wrap small thin pieces of cotton wool around a matchstick, dip into olive oil, and very gently clean the outer ear. DO NOT poke down into the orifice. For ear mites, your vet will be able to supply you with Cooper's P.B. drops.

Fleas and lice: in the best kept kennel these pests will appear, particularly in hot dry weather. All bedding should be discarded if wood wool, and washed if blankets. There are various methods of dealing with this problem and one of the most efficient is ALUGAN made by Hoechst Chemicals. This can be bought either as a powder for shampoo, or in powder form in a sprinkler tin. This must be used fourteen days apart, treating both the coat and the bed.

Ticks: most people know how to deal with fleas but ticks present more problems. Sheep ticks in particular are awkward but if the tick is pulled or broken off, leaving the head under the skin, it is possible it will cause a place that will fester. First dab a spot of petrol, methylated spirit or surgical spirit and almost at once you will be able to pull the whole lot free and clear. I think it gets drunk and then can't hang on. Honest ... I'm serious!

Grass seeds: during the summer months, the grass is dry and the seeds, particularly the wild oat, may get into the dog's ear, the pads or even the anus. An inflammation will be set up and veterinary attention is called for.

Harvest mites: these appear on the best kept dogs in hot summers, particularly on country dogs. A bath of Gammexane (Kurmange), should cure the irritation. These minute red mites can be seen on the stomach, or around the muzzle.

Lameness caused by inter-digital cysts (Digits being the toes): this is in some animals quite common. Glauber Salts from the chemist should be diluted in warm water and the foot soaked in this solution. Repeat this process once or twice daily.

Leptospirosis: two forms of this disease are encountered, the first being Leptospiral Jaundice and the second being Leptospirosis canicola. The former attacks the liver and is contracted from the urine of rats, which causes jaundice and internal haemorrhage and is obviously very dangerous. The latter attacks the kidneys, the infection coming from the urine of an infected dog. Veterinary assistance is needed in either case and the danger from these infections could be avoided by inoculation. Rats should be eliminated from the area if suspected and strict hygiene must be kept. A dog can be a carrier of this disease through his urine for some time after he is cured.

Mange: the Demodetic Follicular variety is unfortunately hereditary in the Smooth and Miniature Smooth Dachshund. The mite burrows under the skin follicles causing the hair to fall out in patches. These patches usually appear on the head and face gradually increasing in size. The body coat grows very thin.

This condition can be dealt with only by the vet. If your Dachshund develops pustules on the body, then an autogenous vaccine can be made, and you should ask (through your vet) for an appointment with the Veterinary College at Bristol.

Sarcoptic mange: the mite in this case causes intense irritation. Some hair will be lost and the skin become dry. Hygiene in both these cases is most important, the dog's bedding being changed and burnt continuously.

Milk after a season: use Epsom Salts, 1 egg-spoonful wrapped in a small piece of tissue paper and gently inserted at the back of the throat.

Parvo virus enteritis: appeared in England in 1979 with a heavy mortality rate. Veterinary opinion regarding the best treatment is still changing and your vet should be consulted for the latest information.

Patchy coats: these can often be caused by loss of condition. Put the dog on to CANOVEL (Beecham Veterinary Products) and give a daily dose of CYTOCON from the chemist. Rub the coat which will probably be dry and scurfy with almond oil. Repeat the oil treatment weekly for a short time. Another method of dealing with lack of coat is to purchase a packet of KURMANGE (Cooper's Veterinary). Bath the dog and follow the directions. A week later, make a smooth paste with some of the powder and apply this to the thin patches on the coat.

To grow a reluctant coat: purchase linseed oil and add two teaspoons of this to six tablespoons of water and simmer very slowly for four hours. Feed daily one teaspoonful. Add one tablespoonful of margarine to the food daily.

Perverted appetites: puppies and older dogs have the unpleasant habit of eating their own and other dogs' excreta. It is probably caused by a diet deficient in adequate minerals. The raw meat ration should be increased and a mineral supplement fed. This can be found in the supplement SA37 which can be obtained through your vet.

Tar on the feet and coat: this can be removed with an application of cooking lard. If on the coat soften the lard slightly and rub with a clean tissue.

Wasp stings: in the canine medicine cupboard should be a bottle of

DANERAL made by Hoechst Chemicals. Give one teaspoonful for every 10 lb body weight, keeping the dog quiet for some time.

Worming: puppies must be wormed, even though the amount of worms vary with different litters. Many preparations are on sale, but to the inexperienced the safest medicine is that supplied by the vet, and given strictly to his instructions; about 3 weeks of age for the first dose. Should the puppies at about this age have very full and tight tummies, it is as well for the vet to have a look at them, as some degree of distension, due to heavy infestation of worms, is often present, and gentle evacuation with a dose of olive oil the previous day, might be necessary.

The temperature of a dog when normal is 101.4, this taken in the anus. If in any doubt as to the dog's health, take the temperature and call the vet if necessary.

Unfortunately Dachshunds as a breed are subject to slipped inter-vertebral discs. The dog will show signs of unwillingness to walk up a step, he may appear restricted in his rear movement, and unsteady when moving. These symptoms may pass within a couple of days, in other cases the ability to move is rapidly lost and the dog registers great pain when the back is touched. The veterinary surgeon must be called and he will give the necessary treatment. In many cases so affected, the dog will gradually improve. Good nursing is essential and great perseverance required on the part of the owner.

17 The Dachshund Overseas

Dachshunds in Australia and New Zealand

'Ch. Silvae Querry turned dogs into Dachshunds'
— the late Jackie Reading

Australian exhibitors have a far larger chance to show at Championship Shows, the number of these being far in excess of what our Kennel Club allocates. If one is determined enough almost any animal can achieve a title, provided one has the wherewithal to travel possibly hundreds of miles. Challenge certificates are awarded on a point system. The largest number of these being on offer at Club Speciality Shows which draw a good entry. The General Championship Shows may be poorly supported, and I realised that a certificate is seldom withheld, and then often by an overseas judge. By our standards there are some cheap Champions.

For the Miniatures there is no weight limit, far too many winning as lightweights at around 14 lb (7 kg). There is now a coterie of exhibitors intent on bringing down the weight to our 11 lb (5 kg).

The Dachshund Club of Victoria's Handbook of Champions for 1975 contains pedigrees for five generations for each dog pictured. It is obvious that the strength of the majority of kennels came from British stock. To mention very few, we find Grunwald, von der Howitt, Silvae, Ashdown, von Weyher, Womack, Cedavoch, Hawkstone, Selwood and Turlshill; many of these occurring in these Australian Champions more than once. As we find over here, both good and not so good can be produced by doubling up on certain pedigrees.

Ch. Silvae Querry and Ch. Womack Wright Royal Show have the largest percentage of winners. The Womacks appear through the Romalos, the Millewas, and the Turins; the Dawkens inbred to him. His daughter Australian Ch. Dawken La Mouche mated to her sire, gave Ch. Vitellius. The Romalos used him extensively, and, through a grandson Ch. Gayhund Remember Me, having winning progeny not only in their own country but in South Africa and Malaysia.

The Millewas in Victoria produce one Champion after another with Millewa Monarch probably topping the lot with innumerable

Aust. Ch. Dawken Vitellius by Ch. Womack Wright Royal Show ex Ch. Dawken La Mouche. Owned and bred by Mr W. D. Archbold.

Aust. Ch. Gayhund Remember Me by Aust. Ch. Lambrigg Too Rite ex Aust. Ch. Gayhund Miss Memory. Owned by Mrs D. W. Batchelor. Bred by Mr L. B. Skinner.

Aust. Ch. Millewa Monarch by Ch. Romalo Wringleader ex Longview Leah. Owned and bred by Mr and Mrs T. Clarkson.

Challenges, Hound Groups and Best in Show. His sire is Ch. Romalo Ringleader (a son of Wright Royal Show), who is the double grandsire of Ch. Millewa Mandalay.

Amongst more recent imports Ch. Silvae Rodney, and now Silvae Clyde are at stud. Mr Hague sent to Mr Hardie, Ch. Limberin Light Laughter, one of the famous 'Laughing' litter. The Millewas mated one of their bitches to him, at eight months a clear red daughter,

Aust. Ch. Lohengrin Sugar Daddy by Ch. Imber Irish Coffee ex Ch. Lohengrin Coffee Crystal. Owned and bred by Mrs Berge Phillips.

Aust. Ch. Garrod
Coffee Mate by
Aust. Ch.
Lohengrin Sugar
Daddy ex Aust.Ch.
Garrod Coffee
Liqueur. Owned
and bred by Mr and
Mrs King.

Millewas Light Gold, won the Challenge at the Hound Show in Melbourne under Mrs Catherine Sutton in 1979.

The Miniatures over the years have imported from Wendlitt, Bowbank, Montreux, and more recently, Hobbithill Yorke of Limberin, who has taken to Australia the most successful combination of pedigrees, Hobbithill and Limberin. In 1977 Ch. Stargang Wurlitzer joined the Sonderbars (grandsire Ch. Merryweather Masquerade).

Aust. Ch. Millewa
Gold Dollar by Ch.
Millewa Gold
Sovereign ex Ch.
Millewa Karisma.
Owned and bred by
Mr and Mrs. T.
Clarkson.

The Miniature Long Hairs have imported a variety of dogs with varying pedigrees – Mertynabbot, Mareth, Sunara. More recently Jackanordie has been represented by two dogs. The background of their pedigrees contains Ch. Mertynabbot Lancelot.

Miniature Wires are not strongly represented, for some reason the wire coat be it Miniature or Standard has not earned the popularity we see here.

The Standard Longs have been to the fore for many years. Mr and Mrs Simon imported in 1964 an Albaney Champion, Red Rock. Like so many of the dogs who had to make the journey by sea, he did not take kindly to those he did not know, and was difficult to show. However he did achieve his Championship and was used at stud frequently. Mr and Mrs Simon followed this import with a second. This time a son and daughter of Ch. Imber Coffee Bean. Mr and Mrs Weston had used Ch. Red Rock and mated his daughter to Australian Ch. Simeon Coffee Bean, doubling up on English Ch. Imber Coffee Bean, through Red

Aust. Ch. Lohengrin Butternut by Ch. Millewa Tobin Bronze ex Lohengrin Taffeta. Bred by Mrs R. Phillips. Owned by Mrs. R. Phillips and Mrs R. Butler.

Aust. Ch. Sonderbar Oh Brandy by Eng. & Aust. Ch. Stargang Wurlitzer ex Aust. Ch. Turin Swy. Owned and bred by Mr W. Hardie.

Rock his grandson. This gave them several Champions. Mrs Berge Phillips who had been breeding Long Hairs for some years, used Australian Ch. Simeon Coffee Bean and bred Ch. Lohengrin Espresso – the top stud for many years. In 1975 Mrs Phillips imported yet another dog from England, this time Imber Irish Coffee, a son of Ch. Imber Hot Coffee and Albaney's Mia Celeste of Imber. Irish Coffee did achieve his title. He too had first disliked the flight and the quarantine. The illustration on page 135 shows his son Ch. Lohengrin Sugar Daddy. Mr and Mrs King of Adelaide have used both of these stud dogs with success, as has Mrs Sherwood.

The Standard Wires have a small following. The principal breeders are Mr and Mrs Robin Hill. They used Culdees Quince (imported by Mrs. Phillips) and bred Ch. Dalton Sea Witch, mating her to another import from England, Australian Ch. Fichtenwald Deister by Ch. Gisbourne Inca. New Zealand has benefited through importations from Silvae over the years – Ch. Silvae Keepsake, Ch. Silvae Withywand and Ch. Silvae Frank. The first two were imported by Mrs Condon, and Ch. Silvae Defender, a Ch. Silvae Virgo son, was imported by Mrs

Aust. Ch. Kerriwen Tru Pride by Chipal Playboy ex Trumond Tamara of Sunkara (Imp. U.K.). Bred by Mrs G. Adolfson. Owned by Mr M. Phelps.

Lightfoot. From this dog came Ch. Ashford Idle Chatter, owned by Mrs Condon, and he has made a great impact on the Smooths. His dam is an Australian Champion, a granddaughter of Australian Ch. Dachswan Phantom and Ch. Silvae Keepsake. A second Ashford Champion is Champion the Hamfatman by Ch. Ashford Alaric by Ch. Withylink, daughter of Ch. Keepsake. Mrs Lightfoot of the Longbays had a lovely red bitch ex a granddaughter of Ch. Defender, Ch. Steady Aim of Longbay.

N.Z. Ch. Ashford Idle Chatter by Eng. and N.Z. Ch. Silvae Defender ex Aust. Ch. Nillbua Sara Jane. Owned and bred by Mrs Condon.

The Miniatures are weighed to our limit, and, I hear, are producing some very typical ones; the Smooths have benefited from the importation of Ch. Willowfield Woodcock from Lady Dick Lauder, his dam has proved her worth as a brood with Champion offspring winning in England.

The Miniature Longs not only have Mr and Mrs Naish, but also Mrs Condon as their supporters.

Aust & N.Z. Ch. Marictur Black Major by Ch. Matzell Midas ex Ch. Marictur Black Modiste. Bred by Mrs M. Turner. Owned by Mr and Mrs D. Hardwick. Exported from England to New Zealand to become an outstanding show/stud dog of the eighties.

The Miniature Wires have great support from Mr and Mrs de Nievelle and Mr and Mrs Brown. The former with mainly Cumtru, the latter with Ch. Silvae Handymouse. The de Nievelles have Standard Wires under their prefix Gold Rush, and added an Andyc to the kennel. Andyc Grand Master was shown also in New South Wales by Mr and Mrs Robin Hill. He is both an Australian Champion and a New Zealand Champion. As in Australia, the Wires do not have the support they are entitled to.

The Standard Longs are few in numbers, and mainly of New South Wales and South African breeding.

N.Z. Ch. Steady Aim of Longbay by Tarkotta Rockfall the Sheriff ex Red Ishtar of Longbay. Owned and bred by Mrs Lightfoot.

Dachshunds in the United States
as seen through English Eyes

American exhibitors set great store on their dogs' showmanship and temperament. The method of presentation is different to that seen here; the animal is on a tight lead, the head held high with the tail held out. The pictures of the Long Hairs show a handsome headed exhibit with lovely small almond shaped eyes. The dogs appear to be large, but I am assured that this impression is caused by a prolific coat.

Many of the Smooths show, for us, an exaggerated forechest with even Champions showing thin flat fleet with slack pasterns. In some cases the second thigh is so lengthy that one wonders just how much push the animal can have from the back feet.

The multiplicity of shows makes it possible, with the aid of a handler,

Can. & U.S. Ch. Braaehaus Traveling Man by Can. & U.S. Ch. Fabeland Blue Chip of Nikobar ex Can. Ch. Braaehaus Royal Ensignia. Owned and bred by Carol and Uffe Braae. Canada's top winning and producing Dachshund of all time – and one of America's top Smooths of the eighties.

U.S. Ch. Han-Jo's Candyman by Ch. Han-Jo's Flaming Flare ex Ch. Han-Jo's Yum Yum. Owned by Beverly Kelly. Bred by Hannelore Heller.

to travel dogs around from show to show collecting points for a Championship. The A.K.C. allot points to every breed on their register for *each* Championship Show – and these run into hundreds. On reading pedigrees one sees Champion after Champion in almost all, and it makes me think that the thrill of making up So-and-So is of little consequence, since it is just a matter of time.

Mrs Howell's Bayards dominate the principal Long Hair winners' ancestry. Ch. Han-Jo's Candyman bred by Hannelore Heller is by Ch. Han-Jo's Yum Yum, she being full sister to Ch. Han-Jo's Ulyssis, who has a number of wins, and was twice Best of Variety at Westminster. Yum Yum was mated to Ch. Han-Jo's Flaming Flare to produce Candyman. This mating produced seven Champions, which even by American standards must be exceptional. A son from this litter Ch. Han-Jo's Cottonpicker was top Dachshund in Canada in 1978, and another litter mate, Ch. Han-Jo's Capricorn was also a consistent Group winner in Canada. Ch. Candyman was the top winning Long Hair for 1978, and almost entirely of Bayard breeding.

For the Smooths I have chosen Ch. Von Relgib's Commandant and Ch. Museland Cybele. As can readily be seen, both excel in outline, bone and hind angulation. The dog is carrying Long Haired breeding on the dam's side and again Bayard appears. Mrs Bigler introduced this breeding as she had an exceptionally good bodied bitch who was lacking in head and in show temperament. 'I could find no Smooth at the time' she says 'whom I felt would give us what we needed. It turned

U.S. Ch. Han-Jo's Ulyssis by Ch. Han Jo's Flaming Flare ex Ch. Han-Joe's Yum Yum. Owned by Ingeborg Kremer. Bred by Hannelore Heller.

U.S. Ch. Von Relgib's Commandant by Ch. Von Relgib's General ex Ch. Von Relgib's Classic. Owned and bred by Ethel Bigler.

out to be a most successful experiment. Since then my Smooths have had exceptionally good heads and their temperament has been consistently marvellous, both in the ring and all other surroundings. By breeding this same Long Hair to one of his daughters (the first Long Smooth cross produced seven in the litter, all of them correctly coated

P. 146

U.S. Ch. Museland's Cybele by Ch. Nixon's Fleeting Encounter ex Am. and Can. Ch. Museland's Alysia. Owned and bred by Mrs Muse.

smooths), we got three top winning Long Hairs. I have not seen reason to try the experiment again, but am considering breeding a lovely Commandant daughter to Ch. Han-Jo's Candyman as I feel he is the best Dachshund of any coat around today, and if we could get the best qualities that both have, we should really have a superb litter.

'The A.K.C. allows us to interbreed coats, and on the litter registration form does not ask the variety. Not until puppies are individually registered does the coat or colour have to be designated and it is acceptable to have all varieties registered in one litter. I have never heard of getting all three coats in one litter, but presently there are a few good-coated Longs coming from Long-Smooth litters, and correct Smooths from the same litter. The same is true of Wires.'

Ch. Cybele shows strong line-breeding to the Marienlust line; this is descended from the von Luitpoldsheims. Erwin of that name appears in our English pedigree as both sire and grandsire of Ch. Zeus von Schwarenberg. Ch. Favorite von Marienlust, the sire of Ch. Falcon of Heying Teckel appears six times in the ancestry of Cybele. In the pedigree of Commandant, Favorite shows six times behind the Heying Teckels.

The Marienlusts made a tremendous impression on the coats of the Smooths, carrying on from one of the Mehrer's foundation bitches who was a granddaughter of Erwin. We had in England a black and tan dog brought over by Mr and Mrs Triefus, Clarion Call von Westphalen. This dog brought back to us another facet of the von Luitpoldsheims. His sire, Ch. Dunkeldorf Gerstmeister went back to Ch. Favorite von Marienlust. The American bred Long-haired dog

Clarion Call von Westphalen by Ch. Dunkeldorf's Gertmeister ex Ch. Penny Candy von Westphalen. Owned by Mr and Mrs Treifus. Bred by Mrs Westphal.

Ch. Han-Jo's 'Xtra Copy L. by Ch. Von Dyck's Mr Bojangles L. ex Ch. Lady Roselyn of Sirius. Bred by Hannelore and Joe Heller. Owned by Kenneth M. Andrews. One of America's top Long-hairs of the eighties.

imported in 1977, Baron Zucker Kaiser, was a grandson of Ch. Hihope Ladies' Man, himself a grandson of the English export to the U.S.A. of Ch. Rose Brocade of Primrosepatch, who was the sire of the big winning Ch. Roderick von der Nidda.

Over the years England has sent to America some good producers. In Long Hairs, Mrs Smith Rewse of the Primrosepatch kennel has sent several which have carried the blood of the German lines which came to England from Germany after World War One. In Standard

U.S. Ch. Vantbe's Draht Timothy who has Ch. Wylde Canasta as grandsire. Owned and bred by Mrs Westphal.

Wires the first to make an impact was Ch. Wylde Canasta, who was much used at stud in the ownership of Mrs Westphal. Ch. Wylde Canasta's outstanding grandson was Ch. Vantbe's Draht Timothy. Some years later Mrs Westphal imported two bitches fron. Mrs Howes of the Broadchecks, so continuing the Wylde line. Mrs Nancy Onthank purchased a nine-month youngster, Pondwicks Hobgoblin, from Mrs Medley. His sire, Moat Hall Mark, was decended from the Wylde prefix, and his dam, Pondwicks Christina, from the Sports line of Sweden. He became a great winner, as did Timothy; and both of them were sires of a multitude of Champions.

In Miniature Longs Mrs Bellamy's Ch. Mighty Fine von Walder added American Champion to his name. Mrs Parsons sent out to the same owner (for Hobgoblin and Mighty Fine were in the same Kennel) a black and tan, Minutist Goliath. When, in time, the progeny of these two Miniatures were mated the offspring did much winning.

U.S. Ch. Pondwicks Hobgoblin by Moat Hall-Mark ex Pondwicks Christina. Bred by Elizabeth Medley in England and taken to America by Nancy Onthank. He became the top-producing Wire and probably had more influence in his country of adoption than any other British Dachshund.

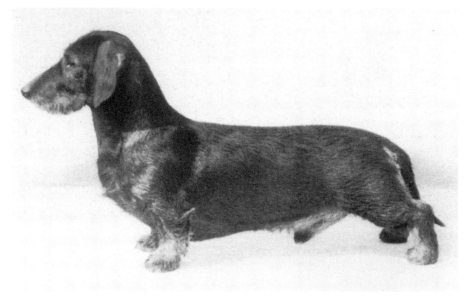

As mentioned in the chapter on Miniature Longs, Mrs Fraser Gibson had sent Sunara Firecracker to the Mays in California. He became a much used dog with many Champion offspring. The Smooths of the Ashdown, von der Howitt, and Selwood prefixes of some many years back, were welded into the pedigrees of the German imports of that time. Coming from the U.S.A. in the late fifties we had amongst others Barton Emanuel and Ch. and American Ch. Jager of Barcedor. This latter dog carried the von der Nidda blood strongly.

As previously mentioned, it is not difficult to make up a dog in the States, for there is an enormous number of Championship Shows, and no points are withheld. Also although there are many owner-exhibitors there are also vast numbers of owners who do have the assistance of handlers.

Ch. Solo's Seafarer W by Ch. Solo's Harbormaster W ex Ch. Solo's Night Song W. Owned and bred by Pattie Nelson. One of the outstanding American Wires of the eighties. (John L. Ashbey)

Dachshunds in South Africa
By Neil S. Kay

Dachshunds are very much a part of South Africa's everyday life, which is quite understandable considering the European countries from which the pioneer settlers came. The South African climate is one of extremes and the heat and humidity nurtures many ailments, in particular skin troubles, caused in part by the myriad varieties of ticks and fleas which abound. Fortunately a sensible routine of bathing the dog every ten to fourteen days in specially prepared 'dips' alleviates these problems. Most Dachshunds love water, so bathing is not a problem. NO it does not ruin coats: in fact, used with conditioners bathing can help to grow coat in the heat of the South African summer.

Dachshunds figure high in the Kennel Union's annual list of registration figures and demand for pet stock is invariably good. In the South African showring, Dachshunds have earned an enviable position of respect by regularly taking high honours at both Group and Best In Show levels and there are many well-known breeders in all varieties, except strangely enough Mini Wires.

Standard Longhairs have been dominated in the last two decades by two kennels, the De Gratton's and the Guntamini's. Neil and Janet Kay's De Gratton kennel has dominated the breed since their arrival in South Africa in 1969, initially started in England from a Benivar bitch mated to an Albaney dog, they have maintained an unbroken line which produced stock which has won over fifty Hound Groups and it is the only kennel to consistently produce Allbreed Championship Best In Show winners. From this kennel came the multiple Group and Best In Show winners, Ch. Galindez, Ch. Duran and Ch. Rocky. In the last decade Claire Paine's Guntamini kennel has become a force to be reckoned with, based on imports from the English Africandawns, the Paines have distributed stock to found other kennels. Foremost amongst these is Chris Hattingh's Africansuns kennel. The Hattingh's campaigned the multiple Group winner Ch. Guntamini Garnette Of Africansuns. Gerhard Robinson established his Nibelheim kennel with the Guntamini pair, Ch. Blaze and Ch. Arianna and imported the bitch Ch. Zigeuner Sieben Mond, a daughter of English Ch. Andyc Mighty Mike. Standard Longhairs in particular are exhibited 'American

Proof of the winning ability of Dachshunds in South Africa. Neil Kay handles S.A. Ch. De Gratton Duran to win the prestigious Natal Top Dog contest, from an invitation field of Group and Best in Show winners.

fashion' with head held high and tails extended, though other varieties are usually handled in the same manner.

Standard Smooths have been the abiding interest of many of South Africa's most talented breeders; overall quality is good and breeders are making progress in eradicating the back problems which bedevil this variety. Bruce Jenkins' Waydach kennel continues to be a dominant

S.A. Ch. Ben Rhydding Bouillet of Lalahapa. A bitch with an impressive show record, including 30 Best of Breeds, 'Lara' is typical of South Africa's type, which falls midway between the English and Continental.

force in the breed, and their many imports have had a positive effect on quality in South Africa. This kennel imported Ch. Sontag Superman Of Ralines a multiple group and Best In Show winner. This dog was mated to Allan Duff's big winning bitch Ch. Ben Rhydding Bouillet of Lalahapa and the offspring show promise to found a successful line. Jill Fox's Foxbournes prove wellnigh unbeatable in the breed, and Ch. Ben Rhydding Rhan Of Foxbourne has become a legend, with over eighty B.O.B.s and fifteen Championship show Hound Groups to his credit. Jill Fox is to be congratulated on her efforts to 'save' the Standard Smooth Dapple and Mrs Fox's endeavours in this regard have been rewarded with two Champions, Ch. Foxbourne Freckles (silver) and Ch. Foxbourne Fynnyon (red).

Standard Wirehairs have, after years of neglect, become more popular, due in the main to the efforts of Mrs M. Mallinger's Vom Igelbau kennels ably supported by Dr and Mrs V. G. Spowart who, after achieving success with Irish Wolfhounds, turned their attention to Standard Wires. Together these breeders have imported the four leading bloodlines in Germany, namely, Dachsslucht, Helvesiek, Gie-sebrink and Tannenbruch. Ch. Igelbau Copa, bred by Mrs Mallinger and owned by the Spowarts, is proving to be the most successful Wire in the South African show ring so far.

There have been many changes in Mini Longhairs in recent years. The kennel which formally dominated the breed, the Jukskeirivers of Mrs Modder Van Gellicum, and the Diminis and Minilands of Chris Rainford and Mrs M. Curtis respectively, whilst retaining their interest in Mini Longs, have tended to concentrate on the Mini Smooths. So a 'new' generation of breeders has sprung up, notable amongst these have been the Ralstons owned by Mrs Carla Nel, who has by the skilful breeding of continental and British bloodlines evolved a recognizable type peculiar to the Ralstons. They all exhibit a dark rich red colour with straight coats and sound toplines. In the Eastern Province city of East London, Mrs Kerry Shultz is evolving a very successful kennel based on Miniland and Dimini, with perhaps Ch. Miniland Magic Eve of Schusborg being the kennel's most successful inmate so far.

Whilst the Mini Longhairs are in a period of change, Mini Smoothairs appear to go from strength to strength, many of its top breeders are centred in the Province of Natal which has a sub-tropical climate, yet despite the heat, with its attendant problems of fleas, ticks and innumerable skin problems, Natal breeders are the breed's current leaders. Mrs Shiela Nel's Morgenster kennel imported Ch. Wimoway Whisky Mac from Scotland, Mac immediately made his presence felt by going Best In Show at an all-breed Championship Show, then topped this achievement by siring Ch. Morgenster Mia Tia, also a Championship Show Best In Show winner. Mrs Modder Van Gellicum continues to produce a series of winning Mini Smooths and a notable newcomer is Mrs Ursula Sottiaux who campaigns fearlessly on the show circuit: Ch. Morgenster Alexander Of Rixensart in particular has been very successful. Chris Rainford maintained her interest by importing Ch. Willowfield Sunray who took two Best In Shows in succession. There are many other breeders of Mini Smooths in South Africa, and the future is bright for this variety.

Showing in South Africa can be difficult, with immense distances between major cities, however, wherever the Hound Group is contested, the Dachshunds by their quality are sure to be in contention and many of them will be home bred as there is no longer the necessity for an import in order to be competitive, thanks to the high standards set by South African breeders.

Appendix 1:
Breed Clubs and their Secretaries

GREAT BRITAIN
The Dachshund Club
Secretary: Dr S. Kershaw,
22 Clee Avenue, Fareham, Hants. PO14 1RR
The Cambrian Dachshund Club
Secretary: Mrs P. Davis,
Dolafon, Valley Road, Ffrith, Nr Wrexham,
Clwyd, LL11 5LP
The Dachshund Club of Wales
Secretary: Miss P. M. Davies,
23 Goodrich Crescent, Newport,
Gwent, NP19 5PE
Eastern Counties Dachshund Association
Secretary: Mrs M. Cross,
17 Burgh Lane, Mattishall, East Dereham,
Norfolk NR20 3QW
East Yorkshire Dachshund Club
Secretary: Mrs P. Hancock,
Birnam House, 40 Harrogate Road, Ripon,
North Yorkshire, HG4 1SU
Great Joint Dachshund Association
Secretary: Mrs R. Gale,
42 Franklin Drive, Grove Green,
Maidstone, Kent
Lancashire and Cheshire Dachshund Association
Secretary: Mrs K. Bethel,
'Lynnewood' 16 Warburton Lane, Partington,
Cheshire, M31 4WJ
Long-Haired Dachshund Club
Secretary: Mrs J. Rowe,
6 Rhoose Road, Rhoose,
South Glamorgan, CF6 9EP
Midland Dachshund Club
Secretary: Mrs F. Winchurch,
Brianolf Kennels, Four Ashes,
Near Wolverhampton
Miniature Dachshund Club
Secretary: Mr J. Boulger,
Rorabuja, 13 Oxford Road,
Horspath, Oxford, OX9 1RT
Northern Dachshund Association
Secretary: Mrs J. Naylor,
Crown Farm House, Dishforth,
Thirsk, North Yorkshire, YO7 3JU

North-Eastern Dachshund Club
Secretary: Mrs G. Gladwin,
11 Kensington Gardens, Eastbourne, Darlington
Northern Long-Haired Dachshund Breeders'
Association
Secretary: Mrs K. J. Shaw,
Mellings Farm, Sourhall Road,
Todorden, Lancashire, OL14 7HZ
Scottish Dachshund Club
Secretary: Mrs J. McNaughton,
Balgownie, Ayr Road, Irvine, Ayrshire
Southern Dachshund Association
Secretaries: Mr and Mrs L. Webster,
Home Farm House, Hodsoll Street,
Nr Wrotham, Sevenoaks, Kent
Ulster Dachshund Club
Secretary: Mrs J. Patton,
31 Ashley Park, Bangor, Co. Down, Northern Ireland,
BT20 5RQ
West of England Dachshund Association
Secretary: Mrs J. Hosegood,
The Hyall, Lyehole, Wrington, Avon, BS18 7RN
West Riding Dachshund Association
Secretary: Mr and Mrs J. Bennett,
Shardaroba, Silverhill Lane,
Teversal, Notts.
Wire-Haired Dachshund Club
Secretary: Mrs A. Kennedy,
5 Pound Lane, Thatcham, Berkshire RG3 4TG

EIRE
The Irish Dachshund Club
Secretary: Mrs W. Jackson,
4 Maritimo House, Blackrock, Co. Dublin

DACHSHUND RESCUE SERVICE
South
Mrs D. Moate,
2 Buttermilk Cottages, Leafield,
Oxon, OX8 5LP (Tel: 099387 541)
North
Mrs V. Skinner,
'Briarfields', 266 Springwood Lane, High Green,
Sheffield, S30 4JQ (Tel: 0742 847425)

Appendix 2: Dachshund Club Awards

In 1966 the Dachshund Club of England offered for competition the Jackdaw Cup, to be awarded to the top winner, all coats, for the highest awards throughout the preceding year. These awards take into consideration not only K.C. Challenge Certificates, but also wins in Group competition, as well as wins of B.I.S. at breed Championship Shows.

Winners are:

Year	Dog	Coat
1966	Ch. Womack Wrightstarturn	Smooth
1967	Ch. Runnel Petticoat	Miniature Smooth
1968	Ch. Rhinefields Diplomat	Smooth
1969	Ch. Delphik Debrett	Miniature Long
1970	Ch. Delphik Debrett	
1971	Ch. Mordax Music Master and	Wire
	Ch. Swansford Brigg of Truanbru	Long
1972	Ch. Swansford Brigg of Truanbru	Long
1973	Ch. Albaney's Red Rheinhart	Long
1974	Ch. Limberin Loud Laughter	Smooth
1975	Ch. Cannobio School Marm	Miniature Smooth
1976	Ch. Drakesleat Klunk Klick of Andyc	Miniature Wire
1977	Ch. Fraserwood Neon Star	Wire
1978	Ch. Phaeland Phreeranger	Long
1979	Ch. Krystona Augustus	Wire
1980	Ch. Turlshill Troubadour	Smooth
1981	Ch. Turlshill Troubadour	
1982	Ch. Pipersvale Pina-Colada	Miniature Smooth
1983	Ch. Pipersvale Pina-Colada	
1984	Ch. Andyc Mighty Mike	Long
1985	Ch. Sutina Barclay Charm	Miniature Wire
1986	Ch. Voryn's Cafe au Lait	Long
1987	Ch. Voryn's Cafe au Lait	Long

Appendix 3: American Breed Standard

GENERAL FEATURES

General Appearance

Low to ground, short-legged, long-bodied, but with compact figure and robust muscular development; with bold and confident carriage of the head and intelligent facial expression.

In spite of his shortness of leg, in comparison with his length of trunk, he should appear neither crippled, awkward, cramped in his capacity for movement nor slim and weasel-like.

Qualities

He should be clever, lively and courageous to the point of rashness, persevering in his work both above and below ground; with all the senses well developed. His build and disposition qualify him especially for hunting game below ground.

Added to this, his hunting spirit, good nose, loud tongue, and small size, render him especially suited for beating the bush.

His figure and fine nose give him an especial advantage over most other breeds of sporting dogs for trailing.

Conformation of Body

HEAD: Viewed from above or from the side, it should taper uniformly to the tip of the nose, and should be clean-cut.

The skull is only slightly arched and should slope gradually without stop (the less stop the more typical) into the finely formed slightly-arched muzzle (ram's nose). The bridge bones over the eyes should be strongly prominent.

The nasal cartilage and tip of the nose are long and narrow, lips tightly stretched, well covering the lower jaw, but neither deep nor pointed, corner of the mouth not very marked. Nostrils well opened.

Jaws opening wide and hinged well back of the eyes, with strongly developed bones and teeth.

Teeth: Powerful canine teeth should fit closely together, and the outer side of the lower incisors should tightly touch the inner side of the upper. (Scissors bite)

Eyes: Medium size, oval, situated at the sides, with a clear, energetic, though pleasant expression, not piercing. Color lustrous dark reddish-brown to brownish-black for all coats and colors.

Wall eyes in the case of dapple dogs are not a very bad fault, but are also not desirable.

Ears: Should be set near the top of the head, and not too far forward, long but not too long, beautifully rounded, not narrow, pointed, or folded. Their carriage should be animated, and the forward edge should just touch the cheek.

Neck: Fairly long, muscular, clean-cut, not showing any dewlap on the throat, slightly arched in the nape, extending in a graceful line into the shoulders, carried proudly but not stiffly.

FRONT: To endure the arduous exertion underground, the front must be correspondingly muscular, compact, deep, long and broad. Forequarters in detail:

Shoulder blades: Long, broad, obliquely and firmly placed upon the fully-developed thorax, furnished with hard and plastic muscles.

Upper arm: Of the same length as the shoulder blade, and at right angles to the latter, strong of bone and hard of muscle, lying close to the ribs, capable of free movement.

Forearm: This is short in comparison to other breeds, slightly turned inwards; supplied with hard but plastic muscles on the front and outside, with tightly-stretched tendons on the inside and at the back.

Joint between Forearm and Foot (wrists): These are closer together than the shoulder joints so that the front does not appear absolutely straight.

Paws: Full, broad in front, and a trifle inclined outwards, compact, with well-arched toes and tough pads.

Toes: There are five of these, though only four are in use. Dewclaws may be removed. They should be close together, with a pronounced arch; provided on top with strong nails, and underneath with tough toe-pads.

TRUNK – The whole trunk should in general be long and fully muscled. The back, with sloping shoulders, and short rigid pelvis, should lie in the straightest possible line between the withers and the very slightly arched loins, these latter being short, rigid, and broad.

Chest: The breast bone should be strong, and so prominent in front that on either side a depression (dimple) appears. When viewed from the front, the thorax should appear oval, and should extend downward to the mid-point of the forearm. The enclosing structure of ribs should appear full and oval, full-volumed, so as to allow by its ample capacity, complete development of heart and lungs.

Well ribbed up, and gradually merging into the line of the abdomen.

If the length is correct, and also the anatomy of the shoulder and upper arm, the front leg when viewed in profile should cover the lowest point of the breast line.

Abdomen: Slightly drawn up.

HINDQUARTERS – The hindquarters viewed from behind should be of completely equal width.

Croup: Long, round, full, robustly muscled, but plastic, only slightly sinking toward the tail.

Pelvic bones: Not too short, rather strongly developed, and moderately sloping.

Thigh bone: Robust and of good length, set at right angles to the pelvic bones.

Hind legs: Robust and well-muscled, with well-rounded buttocks.

Knee joint: Broad and strong.

Calf bone: In comparison with other breeds, short; it should be perpendicular to the thigh bone, and firmly muscled.

The bones at the *base of the foot* (tarsus) should present a flat appearance, with a strongly prominent hock and a broad tendon of Achilles.

The *central foot bones* (metatarsus) should be long, movable towards the calf bone, slightly bent toward the front, but perpendicular (as viewed from behind).

Hind paws: Four compactly-closed and beautifully-arched toes, as in the case of the front paws. The whole foot should be posed equally on the ball and not merely on the toes; nails short.

TAILS – Set in continuation of the spine and extending without very pronounced curvature, and should not be carried too gaily.

Note: Inasmuch as the Dachshund is a hunting dog, scars from honorable wounds shall not be considered a fault.

SPECIAL CHARACTERISTICS OF THE THREE COAT VARIETIES OF DACHSHUND

The Dachshund is bred with three varieties of coat (A) Shorthaired (or Smooth); (B) Wirehaired; (C) Longhaired.

All three varieties should conform to the characteristics already specified.

The longhaired and shorthaired are old, well-fixed varieties, but into the wirehaired Dachshund, the blood of other breeds has been purposely introduced; nevertheless, in breeding him, the greatest stress must be placed upon conformity to the general Dachshund type.

The following specifications are applicable separately to the three coat varieties, respectively:

(A) Shorthaired (or Smooth) Dachshund – Hair: Short, thick, smooth and shining, no bald patches. Special faults are: Too fine or thin hair; leathery ears, bald patches, too coarse or too thick hair in general.

Tail – Gradually tapered to a point, well but not richly haired; long, sleek bristles on the underside are considered a patch of strong-growing hair, not a fault.

A brush tail is a fault, as is also a partly or wholly-hairless tail.

COLOR OF HAIR, NOSE AND NAILS

(a) One-colored Dachshund: This group includes red (often called tan), red-yellow, yellow, and brindle, with or without a shading of interspersed black hairs. Nevertheless a clean color is preferable, and red is to be considered more desirable than red-yellow or yellow. Dogs strongly shaded with interspersed black hairs belong to this class, and not to the other color groups.

A small white spot is admissible but not desirable.

Nose and nails – Black; brown is admissible but not desirable.

(b) Two-colored Dachshund: These comprise deep black, chocolate, gray (blue), and white; each with tan markings over the eyes, on the sides of the jaw and underlip, on the inner edge of the ear, front, breast, inside and behind the front legs, on the paws and around the anus, and from there to about one-third to one-half of the length of the tail on the under side. The most common two-colored Dachshund is usually called black-and-tan. A small white spot is admissible but not desirable. Absence, undue prominence or extreme lightness of tan markings is undesirable.

Nose and nails: In the case of black dogs, black; for chocolate, brown (the darker the better); for gray (blue) or white dogs, gray or even flesh color, but the last named color is not desirable; in the case of white dogs, black nose and nails are to be preferred.

(c) *Dappled Dachshund* – The color of the dappled Dachshund is a clear brownish or grayish color, or even a white ground, with dark irregular patches of dark-gray, brown, red-yellow or black (large areas of one color not desirable). It is desirable that neither the light nor the dark color should predominate.

Nose and nails – As for One- and Two-Colored Dachshund.

(B) Wirehaired Dachshund – The general appearance is the same as that of the shorthaired, but without being long in the legs, it is permissible for the body to be somewhat higher off the ground.

Hair – With the exception of jaw, eyebrows, and ears, the whole body is covered with a perfectly uniform, tight, short, thick, rough, hard coat, but with finer shorter hairs (undercoat) everywhere distributed between the coarser hairs resembling the coat of the German spiky-haired pointer. There should be a beard on the chin.

The eyebrows are bushy; on the ears the hair is shorter than on the body; almost smooth, but in any case conforming to the rest of the coat. The general arrangement of the hair should be such that the wire-haired Dachshund, when seen from a distance should resemble the smooth-haired.

Any sort of soft hair in the coat is faulty, whether short or long, or wherever found on the body; the same is true of long, curly, or wavy hair, or hair that sticks out irregularly in all directions; a flag tail is also objectionable.

Tail – Robust, as thickly haired as possible, gradually coming to a point, and without a tuft.

Color of hair, nose and nails – All colors are admissible. White patches on the chest though allowable, are not desirable.

(C) Longhaired Dachshund – The distinctive characteristic differentiating this coat from the short- or smooth-haired Dachshund is alone the rather long silky hair.

Hair – The soft, sleek, glistening, often slightly wavy hair should be longer under the neck, on the underside of the body, and especially on the ears and behind the legs, becoming there a pronounced feather; the hair should attain its greatest length on the underside of the tail. The hair should fall beyond the lower edge of the ear. Short hair on the ear, so-called 'leather' ears, is not desirable. Too luxurious a coat causes the longhaired Dachshund to seem coarse, and masks the type.

The coat should remind one of the Irish setter, and should give the dog an elegant appearance. Too thick hair on the paws, so-called 'mops' is inelegant, and renders the animal unfit for use. It is faulty for the dog to have equally long hair over all the body, if the coat is too curly, or too scrubby, or if a flag tail or overhanging hair on the ear is lacking; or if there is a very pronounced parting on the back, or a vigorous growth between the toes.

Tail – Carried gracefully in prolongation of the spine; the hair attains here its greatest length and forms a veritable flag.

Color of hair, nose and nails – Exactly as for the smooth-haired Dachshund, except that the red-with-black (heavily sabled) color is permissible and is formally classed as a red.

Miniature Dachshunds

Miniature Dachshunds are bred in all three coats. Within the limits imposed, symmetrical adherence to the general Dachshund conformation, combined with smallness, and mental and physical vitality, should be the outstanding characteristics of Miniature Dachshunds. They have not been given separate classification but are a division of the Open Class for 'under 10 pounds, and 12 months old or over.'

GENERAL FAULTS

Serious Faults – Over or undershot jaws, knuckling over, very loose shoulders.

Secondary Faults – A weak, long-legged, or dragging figure, body hanging between the shoulders; sluggish, clumsy, or waddling gait; toes turned inwards or too obliquely outwards; splayed paws, sunken back, roach (or carp) back; croup higher than withers; short-ribbed or too-weak chest; excessively drawn-up flanks like those of a Greyhound; narrow, poorly-muscled hindquarters; weak loins; bad angulation in front or hindquarters; cow hocks; bowed legs; wall eyes, except for dapple dogs; a bad coat.

Minor Faults – Ears wrongly set, sticking out, narrow or folded; too marked a stop; too pointed or weak a jaw; pincer teeth; too wide or too short a head; goggle eyes, wall eyes in the case of dapple dogs; insufficiently dark eyes in the case of all other coat-colors; dewlaps; short neck; swan neck; too fine or too thin hair; absence of, or too profuse or too light tan markings in the case of two-colored dogs.

A.K.C. Disqualification: Lack of two normal testicles normally located in the scrotum.

Courtesy of
The Dachshund Club of America, Inc.
Member American Kennel Club Since 1895

Index